THE
AUDIOBOOK
BOOK

An audiobook production guide
for indie authors & narrators.

Mad
Mason
Press

RENEA MASON

NOAH MICHAEL LEVINE

ERIN deWARD

THE AUDIOBOOK BOOK
An Audiobook Production Guide for Indie Authors & Narrators
First Edition

Copyright © 2016 by Renea Mason, Noah Michael Levine, Erin deWard.
All rights reserved.

Published by Mad Mason Press
http://reneamason.com/mad-mason-press

ISBN-13: 978-1542726528
ISBN-10: 1542726522

All monetary sums mentioned in this book are in U.S. Dollars (USD)

Cover design by Renea Mason
http://reneamason.com

Edited by Nancy Cassidy at The Red Pen Coach
http://www.theredpencoach.com

Print Interior Layout by Ryan Fitzgerald
https://ryanjamesfitzgerald.ca/book-design

First print edition: January 2017

To our fellow author and narrator friends...
Wishing you much success!

In Loving Memory of Terri Berg.

ACKNOWLEDGMENTS

Thanks to Tammy Becraft, Rissa Blakeley, Haven Cage, Antoinette Hord, Elizabeth Robbins, Dawn Stewart and Karen Tsakos for their time and help.

Thanks to Karen Commins, Debra Holland, Hollie Jackson, Jennifer Kahn, Cherie Lasota, Cyndi Marie, Joc Protho, Lydia Hayden Rella, Gary Solomon, TyDef Media, and the awesome folks at both Audible and ACX.

CONTENTS

INTRODUCTION

Almost everyone knows the famous Chinese proverb from Chapter Sixty-four of the Tao Te Ching, as ascribed to Lau Tzu: "A journey of a thousand miles begins with a single step."

So…here you are, taking your first step on your audiobook journey.

As an author or would-be narrator, the most important questions are: How will you get to where you want to go? And why take us with you?

It's not as though we're terrible company. We do get a little rowdy sometimes—one of us is always cracking jokes, another laughing so hard she snorts, and the third is usually shaking her head at the other two while trying not to laugh, but failing miserably. But who cares if we're the life of the party, you want to know about audiobooks, right?

There are plenty of options. Some books claim you can get rich recording audiobooks on your iPhone, while others charge you $5.00 to convey the same information found on the Audiobook Creation Exchange (ACX)[1] website for free. Some are nothing more than gimmicky sales bibles, professing to make you a bestseller, but are often written by someone who isn't a bestseller. If that's what you're looking for, you won't find it here.

What you will find here is not only the "how to," but also the "why you should" (and sometimes shouldn't) consider particular paths or decisions.

---

1 https://www.acx.com/

As always, we try to have a little fun. How many self-help books ask the question, "Are you comfortable talking dirty into a microphone?" In joining us, you might just glean some crucial information and have a chuckle or two. Most likely at our expense.

We could start by telling you the history of audiobooks, but we know you don't care, and the Wikipedia page has that covered, should you be curious. What we will tell you is our story, one that started out as a simple audition.

In March of 2015, Renea posted a call on ACX for a Duet Narration, which led to more than eight completed audiobooks as a team, an Audie Award[1], a long-term partnership, and this book. We're working on a movie deal too, but David Hasselhoff won't be available to play the part of Noah until sometime in late 2018. We'll keep you posted. *Just kidding.*

We each bring something different to our journey. Noah, an Audible-approved narrator, has performed over 200 audiobooks. Both he and Erin have worked on stage, TV, and film productions. Erin, the founder of a thriving audio description business, also works on Audible projects and has completed more than fifty audiobooks. Since securing her first publishing contract in 2013, Renea has published ten books, including seven independently published titles. Her *Good Doctor Trilogy*[2] and *Symphony of Light*[3] series have collectively won thirteen book awards.

According to a June 24th, 2016, Publishers Weekly[4] article, indie authors using ACX have been nominated for Audie Awards twenty times in the

1 https://www.audiopub.org/winners
2 http://reneamason.com/the-good-doctor/
3 http://reneamason.com/symphony-of-light/
4 http://www.publishersweekly.com/pw/by-topic/authors/pw-select/article/70745-the-state-of-indie-audiobooks.html

past five years, with only three winning their category. We're proud to be one of those three winning teams.

It's not necessarily our experience or Audie win that makes us different, but our relationship. With audiobooks being the fastest growing sector of publishing, we have a unique opportunity to help set the groundwork for what kinds of partnerships are possible in our community. For us, that vision consists of collaboration, strong communication, and mutual understanding between authors and narrators. One of the goals we have for this book is to address subtleties and concepts that might not be so apparent at the beginning of a business relationship, allowing authors and narrators to see both sides of audiobook production. Even though it sounds cliché, we are stronger together—exposing and generating more opportunities as a team than as individuals.

Perhaps we're a little too idealistic, but there have been people who have helped us along the way, and if we put our collective ideas together to help you start your journey successfully, then it's our little way of giving back. We didn't pen this book to sell thousands of copies, though that would be nice. Writing and publishing this turkey took a lot of work, but if we can help others choose the right path for themselves, we'll be contributing to the growth and evolution of an incredible form of entertainment. Plus, it does all of us good if we as a community produce more and better-quality audiobooks. After all, the listening public is hungry for content, but we want their love of the medium to continue to grow. Let's give them what they want.

The bottom line: There's a wealth of opportunity in the audiobook market to explore. In our opinion, collaboration can often lead to better results than individual effort. What follows in this book are processes, hints, suggestions, specifications, questions, and lots of anecdotes about audiobook production. Join us on the journey. Be our collaborators in this unique medium. Help us improve the process and get more people on board. Our jobs as authors and narrators are not easy. Sometimes our work is incredibly frustrating but also very satisfying, expressive, and a *hell-of-a-lot* of fun.

Come on, take our collective hand. We won't bite unless you want us to. ;-)

Renea, Noah, & Erin

AUTHORS' NOTES

Before we begin, we want to address some scuttlebutt that's been heard around the water cooler here at Mad Mason Press.

There's been chatter in the back rooms and dark alleys of the audiobook world and beyond, suggesting listeners of audiobooks, who are also avid readers, are somehow cheating by experiencing books aurally. The notion seems to stem from an idea, proffered by who knows who, that listening to a book, rather than reading it, is somehow a less intellectual experience.

Hmm… We find this notion curious.

This false premise goes so far and so deep that some audiobook "consumers" refer to themselves as "readers," rather than listeners, to avoid the cold stares and cyber-disdain of those wielding the unruly concept like a bully on a playground with a hard, red, rubber ball.

As producers of audiobooks, we can sympathize with those wanting to avoid condemnation. But we are unsettled by the idea they seek to evade. Initially, while writing this book, we tried to be sensitive, choosing "stigma-neutral" terms like audience, target market, consumer, etc. Honestly, it was exhausting, but then it occurred to us that we could be agents of change, destigmatizing the idea and encouraging our audience to embrace the term "listener" with gusto, rather than shame. It is, after all, what they are doing. For that, we are most grateful.

One can no more read an audiobook than one can smell music. It's oxymoronic in a way that surpasses jumbo shrimp, awfully good, and government intelligence. An audiobook recording is composed of sound waves a brain can only process into patterns of recognizable speech by way of the ears. That's how it happens. Ask Bill Nye, The Science Guy!

To those who would suggest that experiencing a book with one's eyes is the only way to fully appreciate and enjoy literature, we say, "BAH!" You may enjoy whatever you like, but judging others for what they like is, well, really judgmental. Even a bully doesn't like a bully.

There is nothing wrong, underhanded, diminishing, or sub-intellectual about listening to art. Nothing.

Art is, of course, subjective in its appeal. The lion's share of books written and audiobooks produced will never wind up on any list of "All-Time Classics." That, our open-eared friends, is OK. Do you like audiobooks about mollusks? Awesome. Do you like shape-shifting frog erotica? You're not breaking any laws. No one has the right to force their taste or preferences upon you.

So for you, the next generation of audiobook producers, we urge you to listen. We encourage you to invite others to listen. With passion and abandon, with wonder, laughter, and tears. Listen with hope. Listen with amazement. But…listen.

Sincerely,

Nay-Nay, Sparkles deWard and BadNoah

The Night Janitors at Mad Mason Press, currently listening to "The Rainmaker" scene in Curing Doctor Vincent. Hubbah HUBBAH!

DEFINING SUCCESS

THE AUDIOBOOK JOURNEY
TERRI BERG

GARY SOLOMON

FINDING MY BLISS

A PERSONAL VISION
BESTSELLER/BIG CONTRACT

NICHE ROYALTY

PUBLISHER'S PET

CRAFT LOVER

NETWORKER

THE AUDIOBOOK JOURNEY

In July of 2016, The Wall Street Journal[1] called audiobooks, "the fastest growing sector in publishing." The fact that you're here, reading this book, shows what a success-minded individual you are, whether you're an author or a narrator. The rewards of the industry can be plentiful, but seizing the opportunity isn't always as easy as it sounds. Like with anything else in publishing and entertainment, the climate of audiobook production is ever changing, and each journey is truly unique.

---

1 http://www.wsj.com/articles/the-fastest-growing-format-in-publishing-audiobooks-1469139910

1

How big is the audiobook industry?

The same WSJ article[1] pegged 2015 audiobook sales at around $500 million—20% higher than the previous year. Those are formidable numbers. According to Audible Customer Service, they have millions of subscribers worldwide and have seen a 40% increase year-over-year. Audible is on track to have 2 billion hours of content downloaded for 2016. That's up from 1 billion hours in 2014. All those listeners are tuning in and turning on to the audiobooks we create!

Since the time *Curing Doctor Vincent,* our first audiobook project, won the prestigious Audie Award for Erotica in 2016, we've been approached by numerous authors and narrators requesting guidance on how to start their audiobook adventure, as well as those already established who were curious about our methods. That demand for knowledge was one of many deciding factors that led to writing this book.

As with any self-help guide, this book is only as good as the commitment and investment you are willing to make. Before starting, you need to understand your own personal vision for success.

Each of us came to audiobook work from different places, with different visions of ourselves and what success meant. We each made choices and decisions that led us to our love of books, and ultimately to each other. We don't know if hearing our stories will help you start yours, but we're hoping they do.

 Terri Berg
Renea ~ *I adore my readers and listeners. There has never been a more supportive group of people to have existed. While*

---

1 http://www.wsj.com/articles/the-fastest-growing-format-in-publishing-audiobooks-1469139910

many have had a major influence on my career, my audiobook journey is solely due to the tenacity, persistence, and wisdom of one person—Terri Berg.

Terri had been a member of my reader group, the Mad Masons, for some time, but she had only managed to read one of my books because she preferred audiobooks, since reading text was difficult for her. She first approached me and tried to convince me to narrate my own books. Voicing my books was not a possibility, because as an indie author, I had already taken on the roles of marketer, webmaster, graphics designer, accountant, publicist, and so many more beyond the writing of the books. Even though I was a voice major in college and no stranger to acting and diction classes, performing my own stories was not something I wanted to consider. I didn't know the first thing about producing audiobooks, let alone narrating them, and had no desire or time to learn.

Terri, however, was determined. When she realized self-narrating was a dead end, and that I felt narration was best left to the professionals, she began prodding me to have someone else produce my books for me. Audiobooks voiced by narrators she liked started showing up in my mailbox, and authors started contacting me randomly to tell me about their experiences with audiobooks.

Terri's hints were not subtle.

One night, after a long conversation, in a moment of weakness, I found myself sitting on the ACX website reading about the process. Several more messages from Terri, and I hit the audition request button.

That audition request led to my contract with Noah and Erin, who I am ever-so-thankful for, and my first audiobook production, Curing Doctor Vincent.

I don't know how long it would have taken me to start my audiobook journey without Terri, but I'm certain you're reading this book today because of her.

Gary Solomon

Noah ~ *In late 2012, just after Hurricane Sandy, I was sitting in a cafe at the end of my block. While I was without power for about ten days, the cafe had re-electrified about two days after the storm. I was sitting there, with my quadruple, decaf espresso, charging my laptop, my phone, my tablet, and who knows what else, looking like a nomadic Best Buy salesperson. Outside the window, I saw a familiar face. I'd known Gary Solomon since I was a teenager. He was, and still is, among other things, a sound engineer who worked at the studio where I first recorded with my band in the early 80s.*

After some initial how've you beens and what's going ons, I asked him what he was REALLY up to. He told me that for the past ten years, he had been working as an independent audiobook editor for Audible, had a crew of engineers and editors working for him, and that it was a great business. He asked me what I was REALLY up to. I had recently moved back to New York after many years away, and I really had no idea what I was going to do. Gary knew I had a background in acting and voice work and suggested I send an audition to Audible.

The thing is, in all my years trying to "make it" as an actor, the idea of narrating books had never even crossed my mind. I was completely ignorant of it. But the more I thought about Gary's suggestion, the more I thought, Holy Crapspackle – audiobooks could be a great thing for me to do.

After my audition for Audible, they gave me one book to do, most likely testing the waters. It was a nonfiction history book about The Civil War. There wasn't much "performing" to be done in this narration. Pretty much a straight read. But I guess they were happy enough, because they gave me more work. Fortunately, that led to more work and discovering ACX and the indie author crew. From there, I learned about editing and mastering, which prompted even more work and great experiences. In short, I found what I deem success.

This chain of events—running into Gary that day, auditioning for Audible, going on to record over 200 audiobooks, working with some wonderful authors—has completely changed my life.

I doubt that I'll ever be wealthy, or that my potential fame will ever reach beyond a small group of really supportive and wonderful listeners. While I'd love to be rich and "known," I am so freaking happy with my life and with what I do. It is extremely fulfilling to earn a living as an actor and producer, and to work with people like Renea and Erin. The team at Audible and all the authors through both ACX and Audible have been great. I can forge my own path, my own destiny. It's a lot of hard work, but you know, most things worthwhile in life do not come without (at least) a little effort.

Finding My Bliss

Erin ~ *I have only ever wanted to act. Ask anyone who has known me since I was a child, and they will tell you my nickname was Sarah Bernhardt (or Madame Butterfly, but that's a different story). I began studying in earnest at age eight and have never stopped. I've acted on stage and in films at different times in my life, but never on a regular basis. In my 20's and early 30's, I had the time to act but not the single-minded focus required. In my later 30's and my 40's, I had a family to support, so I worked in jobs that offered regular paychecks and benefits.*

The jobs I took usually had some element of performance—training, facilitation, public speaking, and the like. In 2007, I found myself working a job I felt particularly ill-suited for, which was primarily writing, and SO not my forte. I began to explore ways I could use my acting without having my face seen. You see, I had convinced myself there was little call for short, round, middle-aged actresses. With the advent of Netflix original programming and other content creators, it turned out not to be the case, but that too, is another story. I eventually found audio description (translating visual images into aural images for people who are blind) and audiobook narration. These two discoveries lead me down one of the most interesting paths I've ever encountered.

I probed for years and studied for more, and then in 2014, I met Noah. Our mutual friend, Emily, introduced us, and he saw me perform with The Strange Bedfellows, a Shakespearean Theatre Company I am lucky enough to be a part of. Noah suggested I look at ACX, which was new to me. I looked. I auditioned. It took awhile, but eventually, I landed my first production. I have never looked back. I am so grateful for what I have gained through my audio work. It's a wonderful way to make a living, and the supportive, creative relationships I've formed have enriched my life beyond measure.

A PERSONAL VISION

IF YOU IMAGINE YOURSELF AS HAVING ACHIEVED EVERY-thing you ever dreamed of from your writing or narration career, what does the picture look like in your mind? Are you wealthy? Famous? Receiving an industry award? When you finally succeed, how will you know? Does the quest for success truly have an end-point?

It's easy to think that everyone has the same answer, but over the years, as we've gotten to know hundreds of writers and narrators, we've realized the answer to this question is as diverse as they are. Not everyone strives to be a bestseller or land a big contract.

Noah and Erin would both love to have one of their audiobook performances praised in The New York Times, while Renea hopes to see her name on the bestseller list of the same publication someday. The bottom line is we each love what we do, but have bills to pay in the meantime. Though the notoriety of The New York Times is one end goal, a big driver for our careers and a measure of success is to keep working, continue to improve at our crafts, and connect with authors and narrators who write and tell compelling stories.

While each vision is unique and goals can change as you achieve each milestone, there are some common themes:

Bestseller/Big Contract

Becoming a bestseller or securing a lucrative contract with a big publisher are probably the most common visions of success for authors and narrators. Beyond generating enough income to sustain a comfortable lifestyle, there's also prestige for each achievement. Setting milestones along the way will fuel the push toward the goal line. Understanding the key driving factor that will propel your career closer to success is almost as important as knowing the destination. In this case, the driver is clearly financial, making success easy to measure.

Niche Royalty

Some authors and narrators only enjoy writing or performing a particular type of story. Niche genres typically have smaller but loyal audiences. Being recognized as a key contributor to the genre or niche is the goal. Unlike the bestseller, where the driver is financial, the niche author or narrator strives for recognition from peers and exposure to their specified genre's audience. This concept does not always lead to sales or sustainable narration work, but many find great satisfaction in writing and performing works they like. Enjoyment of the work is the primary driver.

Publisher's Pet

Some authors and narrators thrive on the idea that another person or company is willing to support and take a risk on their work. For them, that alone is enough. The satisfaction of knowing their work is worth someone else's investment is the ultimate high. Not that they would be upset if their book hit the bestseller list, or if they secured a bigger, better narration gig; they simply have no desire to use their time or resources to drive sales. Publisher recognition is what keeps them working.

Craft Lover

Writers have a passion for writing and actors have a passion for acting, and the idea of diverting attention to anything else is less than appealing, especially working on the business side of things. Their driver is simply putting the words on the page, or performing the work. It doesn't matter if the project makes even a dollar, as long as they have the opportunity to make their art.

Networker

Some authors and narrators build strong connections with writing and voice talent communities. Genres like Romance thrive on interconnectedness. For some authors and narrators, being part of a community, working with others, and the sense of belonging to something greater than their individual work is what keeps them writing or narrating. They aren't driven by sales figures, publisher acknowledgment, or notoriety, but rather by relationships.

Chances are you're a combination of a few of these, or you may be something entirely different. Regardless, understanding your personal vision as an author or narrator will help you choose the right path to producing your audiobook. Defining your driver, a focus that pushes you closer to the goal, will determine the appropriate investment to make.

Ask yourself: Is the decision to make an audiobook in alignment with your vision for success?

Once you understand your vision and what's going to drive you toward your desired destination, it's time to ask why you want to produce or narrate an audiobook. The reason for this decision by someone striving to be a bestseller will be very different than those looking to dominate a niche. While the end decision for most will be to make the audiobook, the "why" may alter the approach to how you proceed. For example, someone on the bestseller path may choose to forgo a publisher contract depending on the terms. Likewise, someone looking for popularity in a niche might seek out a narrator who is in demand with their readership, while someone writing for the love of writing may opt not to produce audiobooks at all.

Even once you've established your path, you'll find it takes longer to get where you want to be if you only have a pair of running shoes versus a car. Resources play a big part in what decisions you make on your journey.

Audiobook production is an expensive endeavor for both the narrator and the author. The amount of time that goes into producing a successful audiobook is at least five times the finished play-time of the book, not to mention the cost of equipment necessary to produce a quality performance. Production rates will reflect that effort and expense, but there are ways to produce audiobooks with limited financial resources at your disposal.

Before we get into more of the ins and outs, let's take a little diversion, a walk on the wild side, if you will, into that ever-mysterious creative part of the brain that drives us to want to write and perform.

THE ART OF AUDIOBOOKS

CRITICAL LISTENING
AUDIOBOOK RESOURCES
AUDIOBOOK EVALUATION
POINT OF VIEW (POV)
NARRATOR GENDER
SPECIAL NARRATORS
NARRATION STYLE
NARRATOR REVIEWS
WARM-UP TIME
DON'T BE A SNOB

THE ART OF NARRATION
DRIVEN TO TEARS
"HI. MY NAME IS RENEA, AND I'M AN AUDIOBOOK JUNKIE."
NARRATING FICTION
WE HAD A THREE-WAY
NARRATING NONFICTION
SEEMED LIKE A GOOD IDEA AT THE TIME
NONFICTION FRICTION

TODAY'S AUDIOBOOK ENTHUSIASTS WANT MORE FROM audio productions than simply someone reading words. They want a performance.

While most of us are not Pulitzer Prize-winning authors or Oscar-winning actors, we still have our job to do in creating something special and prefer to have fun while making a living at the same time. So, now that you have examined your personal definition of success, it's time to learn the secrets behind the magic we seek to create.

We say magic, because what seems as simple as reading a book, is actually a complicated convergence of talents—acting, writing, engineering, marketing, project and people management, computer and technical skills, and business acumen. As with any successful business, the foundation is a solid product, and in this case, the art behind your audiobook will support everything else you do. Whether you're looking to land a publishing contract, gain recognition in your genre or industry, or are heading straight for The New York Times Bestseller list, investing in yourself will make your road to success much easier.

As you may have guessed, the art, your building blocks, will be composed of two parts—the writing and the performance. The relationship between author and narrator is co-dependent. Listeners have said a mediocre, or even a less-than-mediocre, book can be an incredible audiobook with the right narrator. They also pointed out that a sub-par narrator can kill a stellar book. If you read reviews of audiobooks, you may notice that people will sometimes blame bad writing on the narrator and blame a bad performance on the author. In reality, an excellent performance is the marriage of the narrator to the text.

It's likely, if you're an author reading this book, you already have a manuscript published and are waiting to give voice to it, but it's equally possible you're someone seeking to become a narrator or a narrator looking to hone your best practices. No matter why you ended up in the pages of our little book, it's important for both sides of the partnership to understand the other to foster better collaboration, make more informed choices, and produce better-quality audiobooks.

CRITICAL LISTENING

JUST LIKE WRITING, AUDIOBOOK PERFORMANCE AND production is an art. As with any art form, taste is a factor, so understanding what types of performances you like will help make your production a better representation of you and your work. By listening to audiobooks, you will get a feel for the different stylistic options. As either an author or a narrator, immersing yourself in the industry in which you'd like to work will help you learn what best practices sound and feel like, and determine whether this art form is a good match for your goals and abilities. So, charge up your device, put on your headphones, and prepare to listen to some audiobooks.

Audiobook Resources

Buying numerous audiobooks can be an expensive undertaking since full retail, non-Audible-member pricing can go up to around $25 per audiobook, but there are many inexpensive ways to accomplish your goal. Don't exhaust your budget for producing an audiobook on buying audiobooks at full retail cost.

- ▶ Reach out to authors for free codes in exchange for an honest review.
- ▶ Sign up for service with Audible. They have a 30-day free trial and discount pricing for members.
- ▶ Check to see if your local libraries carry audiobooks.

Audiobook Evaluation

As you listen, take note of what you like about the performances, and what you wouldn't want to hear in your own production. What worked? What made listening difficult? Were the accents and opposite gender voices believable? How was the pacing? Was the narration robotic, expressive, or melodramatic?

Even though, as authors and narrators, you each have your own styles and would be hard pressed to copy another's, understanding your preferences surrounding audiobook narration will allow you to communicate what you want in a performance or seek out the training necessary to improve your craft.

Select several and critically listen while considering the following items.

▶ Point of View (POV).
▶ Narrator Gender.
▶ Special Narrators.
▶ Narration Style.
▶ Narration Reviews.
▶ Warm-up Time.

Point of View (POV)
Point Of View, the perspective an author uses to tell a story, can make a difference in the feel of an audio performance. There are distinctions within first and third person storytelling that further clarify the way author expresses the story, but for now you only need to be concerned with the general concepts.

A story told from first person perspective gives an intimate view of the character's thoughts, but a very limited line-of-sight into the story action. The main character is the story narrator in this case. As a reader, you view the plot as it unravels through the eyes of one character at a time, while they tell the story using pronouns like "I," "me," and "my." Renea's Symphony of Light Series and The Good Doctor Trilogy are all told in first person POV.

In third person perspective, a story narrator follows the characters, informing the reader of the events as though the narrator watched the character's actions unfold. These stories typically use pronouns like "he," "she" and "they," and have a broader view of the story events.

Some stories alternate between POVs from chapter to chapter. One of the best ways to determine a book's POV is to read the sample chapters available at major retailers like Amazon or ask an avid reader or audiobook listener.

Even though neither perspective is especially preferred and both make for fabulous audiobooks, there is a different feel to each viewpoint. Listen to understand the distinctions, so you're equipped to make better decisions when it comes to selecting a narrator or project.

Narrator Gender
Since you're listening to gain perspective for either your book or career, listening to performances by both men and women can be helpful, but getting a feel for narration that matches either your gender or a character's gender will give you the most insight. Understanding how a female narrator successfully performs male voices or vice versa can provide great perspective.

Special Narrators
Listening to celebrity-narrated books may not be the best use of an author's time in figuring out how to produce their audiobook. These productions usually have larger budgets than the typical indie author or narrator will have at their disposal. While celebs sell a lot of audiobooks, getting one to narrate yours is unlikely.

Full-cast production audiobooks, using more than two actors, can be great fun, but again, probably not something a typical author would undertake for their project.

Also, steer clear of books narrated by the book's author, since you will most likely not be narrating your own book, and this type of narration creates a unique experience.

Narration Style

Narration comes in a variety of styles—Solo, Dual, Duet, and Full-Cast. Assess whether the story has one or multiple narrators. The style of narration can change the feel of a book. Sampling a variety of books might open your eyes to the idea of narrating with a partner or choosing more than one narrator for your project.

Narrator Reviews

After choosing your titles, check the narrator reviews on Audible. Pick books with rave narration reviews and others with struggling or mixed reviews. Take notes, and then compare and contrast the differences. What does the audience say about the performances? What did they like or dislike? Did you agree with the reviewer's assessment?

Warm-up Time

If you're new to audiobooks, it's important to point out that most performances, even by very accomplished narrators, have a bit of a warm-up period, taking a chapter or so before the narrator and the story mesh. This delay could be because the narrator needs some time to settle into the characters, or because the story takes time to settle into a rhythm, or simply because as the listener, you might be expecting something different in your head. Even when reading the book before recording, narrators don't usually have time to rehearse. Now that you know, try not to give up on the narrator in the first few chapters. Often their performance will grow on you, and then you won't be able to imagine the book without them. It's a common occurrence to be unsure for the first few chapters, especially if you are new to listening.

Once you've listened, get others to evaluate the same books and see if they come to the same conclusions. People who regularly listen to audiobooks are great assets. You may have your own opinion of what's good and not so good, but you're not the only one buying audiobooks. Ask readers, friends, and family, or anyone who are avid listeners for their opinions.

Don't Be a Snob

Renea ~ *I've listened to a ton of audiobooks. Hundreds of audiobooks. That's one thing that makes me somewhat unique. I was a keen listener long before I thought of writing, let alone making audiobooks. Time for a confession. Once upon a time, I was a bit of an audiobook snob. You know that friend that will only drink micro-brewed or imported beers? That's how I was with audiobooks.*

I was super picky about my narrators. Maybe it was because I was a voice major in college, but the tone and timber of the narrator's voice had to be right. If I found someone aurally pleasing, I'd listen to all of their books, so that I didn't have to risk disappointment.

The problem I ran into was there weren't as many audiobooks back then, and my library became filled with books I never finished. Out of desperation and a dwindling bank account, I was forced to go back to those books that never made it past chapter two through my car speakers.

I discovered something interesting. When I started to listen the second time, since I knew what to expect and how the narrator would sound, I didn't have the same knee-jerk reaction and was able to settle into the story. I also discovered that some narrators need a little time to meld with the story. Some of the books that sat in my original "did not finish" pile, upon second listen, became some of my favorites, along with the narrator.

So the first lesson here? Don't be a snob. The second? Don't judge a narrator by their first few chapters.

THE ART OF NARRATION

MAYBE YOU'VE BEEN TOLD YOU HAVE A GREAT VOICE. Perhaps you love to read bedtime stories to your kids. It's possible you think audiobook narration sounds like a fun, easy way to make money, or you're an author thinking of adding voice to your own book while wondering, "How hard can it be? It's just reading, right?"

You may have a great set of pipes, or be excellent at character voices when you read aloud, but these traits don't necessarily make a great, good, or even mediocre narrator. Many authors who self-narrate their own books come to regret the decision, both during the production process and after finishing the audiobook.

What makes good narration?

Engaging narration is evocative and immersive. More than good diction, a pleasant voice, and an ability to talk for exceptionally long periods of time, a skilled oral storyteller catches and holds the attention of the listener, conveys the emotions of the characters within the framework of the story as written by the author. This ability brings the listener into the present and compelling journey of the story. In a nutshell, audiobook narration is acting.

Wait. What? Audiobook narration is just like standing on stage or being on camera? It is.

The only ways in which audiobook work differs from stage, TV, and film acting, other than the fact no one can see your beautiful face, is the amount of time you are performing and that there is usually no rehearsal. It is also very intimate acting, with your voice reaching right inside the listener's head. The most well-loved and sought-after narrators connect listeners in a visceral and essential way to the stories they perform. They do this by finding the actable emotions in each scene of the book and tempering their performance by creating a personal and private space for their audience. They have to sustain this connection for the full running time of the book of five, ten, or even twenty or more hours.

It's not always easy to quantify, but when you hear a narrator connect with their work, you just know it. How that happens can be different for each performer or listener. It's the difference between thinking, "My, she has a lovely voice," or having to pull off to the side of the road because the audiobook you're listening to left you sobbing, laughing, or so aroused you can no longer drive.

The narrator's connection to a book is just as real for nonfiction as it is for fiction. A skilled nonfiction narrator channels the author, knowing what they have to share with listeners is the most fascinating information, even when, arguably, it might not be. They do not fall back on using a National Public Radio voice to convey gravitas or read as if they are performing a soliloquy from Hamlet. They slip into the text, letting the author's voice lead them, which can be a daunting task. Not every book, fiction or nonfiction, is written with the same level of passion and emotional investment. It's the narrator's job to take the characters, situations, and story seriously. This nuance can make or break a book.

19

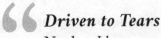

Driven to Tears

Noah ~ I have, many times, been deeply moved by the material I've narrated. Emotions ranging from pure joy to terrible sadness to absolute outrage have welled up in me, both performing fiction and nonfiction. There were times I had to stop recording because I broke down sobbing.

Many of the nonfiction books I've recorded have been more of a detailing of facts than a passionate plea. There's nothing wrong with sharing facts dispassionately, but as an actor, there's more to dig into with material that "takes a position."

A few years ago, I recorded several books that either directly, or tangentially, talked about the assassination of JFK. Recently, I narrated one about the assassination of Martin Luther King, Jr. Several of these books were so passionately written that I was totally pulled in. I felt the authors' sense of anger, incredulity, and dismay through their detailing of events. Their painstaking research revealed webs upon webs of deceit, disinformation, and denial of what seem to be very clear facts and an overall sense of the cover-up of the truth. Writing with this much heart and personal investment can provide an actor with a broad and multi-colored palette from which they can draw to paint the story for the listener.

I have been moved to tears many times in my work. Just as much in nonfiction as in fiction. For me that is an actable emotion.

"Hi. My name is Renea, and I'm an Audiobook Junkie."

Renea ~ It's true. I reconnected with my love of reading after the birth of my first child, wearing out a Kindle or two. But when son

20

number two arrived, there was no time to read. With two little boys only twenty months apart, and a demanding career with a two- hour commute, the day I discovered audiobooks, my life was changed forever. As a process expert in my other life, the idea of enjoying my favorite authors while folding laundry, making dinner, or driving to and from work made me downright tingly.

It didn't take long to realize that not all narrators are created equal. Some neither enhance nor stand in the way of the story. Some make you want to ram pencils into your ears. Still others could be a substitute for over-the-counter sleep aids. Yet some bring out nuances in the author's work that simply aren't felt reading the words on the page, giving the story an extra dimension and adding to the enjoyment, just like my fabulous partner, Erin deWard. On rare occasions, you'll find a narrator that can melt your panties right off even on the coldest winter day; there's a reason they call Noah Michael Levine the #auralsexpert.

The best thing about audiobooks as opposed to movies or TV is that you don't lose any of the elements of the story, and the characters are always the perfect representation of what the author wanted you to see, because it's your mind that fills in the blanks, not a film or TV director. It was the incomparable Stephen King who said, "Description begins in the writer's imagination, but should finish in the reader's." In my opinion, when you have a good narrator and author, audiobooks intensify this phenomenon.

As you might imagine, after listening to hundreds of audiobooks, when I set out to make my own, I had high expectations.

Audiobook narration is the kind of work one does for long stretches of time, both on a given day and within the scope of how long it takes to record a whole book. It is both physically and emotionally taxing. It's solitary acting, which is often conducted with no feedback or other human interaction, and usually performed without a director, colleague's input, or applause.

It's demanding acting where the narrator must develop multiple characters with little to no rehearsal, and be able to maintain their distinct voices, especially in scenes where more than two or three characters speak to each other, sometimes across multiple books in a series. The voice of "Declan" has to sound the same in book five as he did in book one.

Male narrators may have to voice multiple believable women and children without sounding like a helium-sucker. Female narrators may have to portray men who all sound different and don't sound like thirteen-year-old boys—unless they're playing thirteen-year-old boys. Regardless, it's seriously fun acting!

There are two major camps when it comes to voicing characters in audiobooks—those who want a narrator to use distinct voices for each character and those who want the writing to make the differentiation.

Narrating Fiction
Just because a narrator gives each character a different voice doesn't necessarily make it a good performance. Voices chosen with some kitschy idea behind them—for instance, a dragon that sounds like a cartoon character—can be distracting and disconnect the reader from the story. The dragon doesn't know he's a dragon; he just knows how he feels. Because of this, ensure characters are taken seriously and acted from a place of believable emotion, regardless of whether they are a dragon, a bandit, or a tree stump.

Anyone who has ever taken an acting class knows about actable emotions. You can act angry, but you can't act lost. In order for the performance to be believable and engaging, the narrator needs to be able to name the emotion each character (including the omniscient narrator, if there is one) is feeling and then act it. We've all seen movies where the people on screen are not believable. It isn't because they're witches or demons, talking sausages, or any character, but rather because they are phoning it in, speaking the lines but not acting the emotion.

The choices you make as a narrator can take the text in any variety of directions, so be very clear about understanding how the characters are written. An author will describe a character's emotional state, and you'll have to find a behavioral arc to make the descriptions authentic.

We Had a Three-Way

Renea, Noah & Erin ~ *When the three of us began work on The Good Doctor Trilogy, we had many discussions about character voices. Vincent and Elaine were fairly straightforward in their depiction. She's a strong woman, so Erin went with a solid, bold voice. Xavier had to sound intelligent and sexy, but also vulnerable. The real fun came in working out the other characters. Marco and Sebastian had to sound very different from Xavier, but also had to be leading men in their own right.*

Marco was Italian and a class clown of sorts, so his tone needed to be more playful. Sebastian, a Frenchman, was at first the strong silent type, with an affinity for nipple twisting. The character of Victoria, Elaine's nemesis, was totally fun because her tone was deep, breathy, and seductive, and a total bitch. Miriam had to be French, sickly, but also resonate with a little bit of sexy sparkle and be very much in love with Sebastian. What was cool about

Sebastian was that his role became more prominent in each book, so his voice grew more firm and determined. We hashed all of this out together, and it was both challenging and exceedingly fun.

Narrating Nonfiction

Channeling the author's emotional tone is the key element to any well-performed narration. Some nonfiction authors will write passionately about their subject, which could be anything from a scientific discovery to politics and literature. Memoirs also fall into this category. The tone of the book may sometimes decide the performance style for the narrator, especially when the author has strong opinions and feelings regarding their topic.

However, some nonfiction is without a specific tone. It might seem to be a dispassionate telling of facts or events. It can be tricky to infuse "acting" into this type of narration, but if you adjust pacing and cadence, presenting the information as the most fascinating set of facts you've ever had the pleasure to share, without going overboard, you can offer the listener more than a dull recitation.

As for quotes from well-known people, in most cases, you are best served by not trying to mimic or approximate anyone's voice. You may do an awesome Angela Merkel or Ben Bernanke, but within the context of nonfiction, the emotional content of the quote is what is important. Trying to sound like Sigmund Freud, when you're not, in fact, Sigmund Freud, will probably earn you more bad reviews than good.

Seemed Like a Good Idea at the Time

Noah ~ *Very early in my career, I did a 34.75-hour book about the German philosopher Hegel. It was, I believe, a doctoral-level tome, written by over twenty contemporary philosophers. I thought, "Wow, whoever listens to this will be hearing my voice* in their ears a lot. I should find a way to mix it up a little." So, when there were actual quotes cited from Hegel or one of his contemporaries, I used accents, mostly German or British. Now, I keep hearing how good I am at doing accents, and maybe I've improved some over the past few years, but after reading reviews of that audiobook, ha-ha, um... They were not well received. "Cartoonish" was one word used to describe my efforts. Not really appropriate for a serious discussion of one of history's best-known philosophers.

Likewise, in a book about the politics of vodka in Russia, at times I used Russian accents while narrating quotes. Now, I lived among the Russians of Los Angeles for four years, and I think I do have a pretty good ear for accents. I felt the sounds coming out of my mouth were realistic, based on my real-life experience. But reviewers felt otherwise. One review was titled, "Look, Natasha, Moose and Squirrel are drunk!"

My failures shouldn't dissuade you from giving it your best shot, and I use accents all the time in my work, usually with more success than failure, but remember that if yours are not authentic, you might get that sinking feeling when reading your reviews.

Nonfiction Friction

Erin ~ All I'm going to say here is that nonfiction can be much harder than fiction. Some people have a real knack for it, but I find it super hard. I've done a few. I recognize it isn't a strength of mine, but I keep studying and working on it. Two of my "favorite" reviews for one nonfiction title are: "Narrator is THE WORST MOST ANNOYING ever!!!" and "The narrator sounded like she just got beat and let out of her cage for the first time in her life. What a horrible reading." Just to be clear, I was reading this *book as if I was the person who had written it, giving it all of my attention, and presenting it as the most stimulating material available, which it kind of was. Nonfiction is a unique beast, and it takes a special kind of delivery for it to be what the author intended.*

After discussing why character voices can help channel the tone and voice of a story, please note there are some who believe there should be no character voices in either fiction or nonfiction. These people—authors, seasoned narrators, and listeners who leave reviews—feel audiobooks are a different breed with their own performance modality and narrations not differentiating voices in any marked way. They loathe an "acted" book, preferring the book be simply read. Their opinion is a matter of taste, but with the industry producing more and more multi-narrator and full-cast, fully-acted audiobooks, this style isn't as popular as it once was. Some companies, like Pocket Universe, even record on location with ambient noises like one might experience in a movie.

Regardless of style, if you want to be a narrator, you need to train in acting and narration. Beyond honing artistic skills, if you're looking to make a career of audiobook narration, you still need to learn how to use recording and editing software, self-direct, and run a business for real success. You can't skip any of these steps as you'll be competing with people who have years of experience perfecting their technique.

Narrating is fun, but it's also lots of hard work and many long hours. There is no quick and easy path, but if you're up for the challenge, it can be a wonderful way to make a living.

THE BUSINESS OF AUDIOBOOKS

THE BUSINESS OF NARRATION
TIME
RECORDING
EDITING AND MASTERING
RECORDING SPACE
OUT OF THE CLOSET AND INTO THE BOOTH
FROM DRAPES TO WALLS
EQUIPMENT
LET'S TALK ABOUT MY EQUIPMENT
MY FAVORITE SET OF HEADPHONES—A LOVE STORY
QUICK DAW MCGRAW

THE BUSINESS OF PUBLISHING
ACX DISTRIBUTION
PUBLISHING OPTIONS
INTERNATIONAL OPTIONS
A CORNUCOPIA OF CHARACTERS

THE ECONOMICS OF AUDIOBOOKS
FRONTEND CONTRACT
BACKEND CONTRACT
HYBRID CONTRACT
PER FINISHED HOUR (PFH)

27

ROYALTY SHARE (RS)

ROYALTY SHARING IS CARING... AND DARING

STIPEND

HYBRID CONTRACT

SELF-EMPLOYMENT

SAG/AFTRA

FEES AND ADDITIONAL COSTS

ROYALTIES

WHISPERSYNC

BOUNTIES

———————

NOW THAT YOU HAVE A BETTER FEEL FOR THE ART OF audiobooks, let's put on our business-casual best and get into the "other" side of things. It may not be as sexy, but it's definitely as important. Having your wits about you will be vital, no matter your vision, since there will be significant expenditures of time and money for both the author and narrator throughout the process.

THE BUSINESS OF NARRATION
Time
If you're an aspiring narrator, you need to decide how much time you're able to devote to this endeavor, and whether or not narrating/producing audiobooks will be a full-time career, a second job, or a hobby. Authors have to make similar decisions before taking valuable writing time to listen to loads of auditions, ensure their manuscript is well edited for audio, and to review each chapter of the audiobook before signing off on the performance, but their time commitment will pale in comparison to yours on this leg of the journey.

Start by considering how many hours a week you can put into

recording, editing, and mastering. How much time are you willing to devote to auditioning for projects you won't get? There's much to ponder, so let's start with how much time it can take to record an audiobook. For this discussion, let's use an audiobook with a final run-time of ten hours as our example.

Recording

On average, a ten-hour book can take a narrator anywhere from fifteen to twenty hours or more to record. Some people may be faster, and some slower. You might be going along great for a few minutes and then get stuck on one word or sentence that takes you five or ten minutes to get right. That adds up over time. Some text will flow smooth as fine sippin' whiskey through your eye-brain-mouth connection; others may have you stumbling around like you drank too much tequila. Each book is different.

Editing and Mastering

It can take another fifteen to twenty hours, or more, to edit and master—the process that removes errant sounds, tightens pacing, and ensures a quality product—a book. There are two options for this phase: "DIY" (Do It Yourself) or "FIO" (Farm It Out). One costs time, the other, money. Some might argue, however, that time *is* money.

Going the DIY route saves dough, allows one to gain proficiency in editing and mastering, and centralizes control over the quality and consistency of sound. FIT frees up considerable time, which enables you to take on more projects, puts the execution of some pretty technical stuff in the hands of a professional, and allows another set of eyes and ears to review the performance, which is almost always a good thing.

In either case, editing and mastering involve:

▶ Listening to the entire book, perhaps more than once
▶ Removing errant noises—pops, clicks, the occasional dog bark, etc
▶ Ducking (toning down) loud breaths or covering extraneous breath sounds with "room tone"
▶ Quality Control (QC) to make sure the narrator hasn't made any reading or pronunciation mistakes. This includes applying mastering effects, such as leveling, EQ, compression, normalization, and noise reduction to make sure the files meet ACX requirements

Authors understand each and every one of these steps. They apply them, in another sense, to the books they write. They, and an editor they hire, go through the book many times, fixing typing mistakes, misspelled words, and checking grammar and punctuation—the pops and clicks of writing. Those "mastering effects" such as cover design, typeset, and layout all have to be applied to a book before it is set free upon the world.

No matter how much you, as a narrator, love a book, the author's writing, or your performance, editing and mastering can be a very time consuming and tedious process. However, paying a post-production professional can take a fair chunk out of your wallet. Audio editors charge in the neighborhood of $75 Per Finished Hour, depending on what they are providing—editing, quality control, mastering. You will need to decide if you have the time to learn the art of editing and mastering or if it makes sense to pay a trained professional. Most career narrators pay someone. Regardless, at some point, if you're serious about narrating/producing, you're going to need to get in there, roll up those sleeves, and get your hands, or rather ears, dirty.

In total, narrators could be looking at thirty to forty, or more, hours' worth of work for a ten-hour finished audiobook.

Time. Time. Time. It's important to consider.

Recording Space
Let's face it; no one wants to hear a lawn mower, a truck rumbling by, or the sound of footsteps on a wood floor while they're listening to an audiobook. While the exception would be an audiobook production that includes real-world sounds, that is not the rule. So, your recording space is a crucial aspect of your business.

Renting someone else's studio or booth space is, in most cases, too costly and inconvenient for it to be an effective, ongoing production model. Even if you don't have to pay an engineer, the cost for space coming out of what you make at the end of a project, considerably reduces your income. While building your own "studio" sounds daunting and expensive, and in some cases, it can be; it doesn't need to be. There are lots of innovative and inexpensive ways to carve out a quiet place to make the magic happen.

There are all manners of ways to create an acoustically appropriate space—blankets, different types of padding, partitions, etc. Search the Internet for "creating a recording space in your home," and you'll find pages of information that will help you figure out what works for your budget.

We can't stress enough that having a quiet space is of paramount importance for creating a high-quality audiobook. Even though some background noise is eliminated when your audio files are "compressed" through the ACX system, we all want our projects to sound as close as possible to those coming out of the major audiobook production companies. Part of your reputation will be dependent upon the quality of your recordings.

Out of the Closet and into The Booth

Noah ~ Erin and I took two different approaches to "building" our recording spaces. I started out in a walk-in closet and endured many jokes about coming out of it. It wasn't large, but it was big enough for a small desk to hold a microphone, a mouse, keyboard, and a tablet. A computer monitor was ensconced in an open drawer of a built-in dresser. There was carpet on the floor, clothes hanging all around, and a closable door. It was a pretty good setup for what I needed. A couple of years later, I moved to a place that had no such closet in which to set up shop. There were wood floors, high ceilings and a lot of potential for sound to bounce and echo. I wound up buying a sound booth, and with the help of a couple of friends, put it together in my office. The booth came in twenty separate boxes. My apartment is on the top floor of a three-story walk-up. So, yeah, that was fun. But the booth is great. It doesn't block out ALL sound, but it does a good job of keeping me in a very quiet, contained environment. Plus, it's big enough for two or three people, so, we can have a lot of fun!

From Drapes to Walls

Erin ~ My path from open space to booth started out with hanging heavy drapes and blankets over PVC frames in a section of my bedroom. I used pillows and towels around a folding table to dampen sound. I purchased a package including a mic, mic stand, shock mount, a small pre-amp, and a pop-screen. I worked on a laptop I borrowed from work. Shhh—don't tell. While it was sufficient to get me going, it wasn't what I really wanted.

When we moved into a new house, there was a tiny office on the second floor. I took all of my drapes and blankets and hung them in there, and bought a Mac Mini and an external storage drive. Again, it worked, but the sound was not as professional as I wanted. I did a lot of research and began to visualize what I did want. Finally, over the course of many months, my husband and our friend, Ken, built my booth-within-a-room.

In both my and Noah's cases, the total cost was about the same, but the situations were different and so different solutions were needed. Neither is perfect. My dogs still bark, motorcycles still rev up and down the street from time to time, so I have to stop recording and wait for the noise to pass. Each of our solutions represents a considerable investment of time and money. But it's what we needed to do our jobs and create our art.

Equipment

What do narrators need to produce a good-quality audiobook? Contrary to popular belief, you really can't do anyone's writing justice recording on your iPhone. There's a person out there selling books and audiobooks about making millions doing just that. We're not saying it can't be done, but you know, it can't be done. Or if it can, it probably shouldn't.

That said, you don't have to mortgage the house to get set up. Here are some of the things you will need:

- ▶ Desktop or laptop computer to record audio files.
- ▶ Software to record, edit, and master audio files.
- ▶ Tablet for reading PDFs.
- ▶ A decent-quality microphone.
- ▶ Headphones (if preferred).
- ▶ A pre-amp/interface of some kind (maybe).

- ▶ A wind/pop screen.
- ▶ A place to plug in all this stuff.

Most up-to-date desktop and laptop computers will work just fine, however, processor speed, the amount of memory, and storage can affect the performance of equipment and software. Many people record using a laptop, but be aware, if the computer is in the "booth" with you, you run the risk that recordings may contain computer fan noise. With a desktop computer, the monitor and CPU can be in separate places, keeping the fan noise outside of the recording space.

Some people will tell you, "Dude, you have to use a Mac. You have to use a Neumann microphone. You have to use Pro-Tools!" You don't have to use any of those things. Whether you use the most expensive equipment/software available or more moderately priced alternatives, the quality of your audiobook may be indistinguishable regardless.

A microphone must sound great with your voice. Crazy right? Not every type of mic blends well with every type of voice. Here is another necessary time and financial investment. In the best of all worlds, you will try out several different kinds of mics and choose the one that, when you listen to yourself on a recording, sounds warm and present, with the right balance of bass and treble. Most brick & mortar and online retailers have lenient return policies, but do check them out before you buy.

There are two types of mics to consider: A USB mic, which plugs directly into your computer or a "condenser" mic that will need to connect via an interface of some kind, such as a pre-amp or mixer.

USB mics vary in price, but a decent recording one will cost at least $100. Do your research, as many of these mics do not produce audio that is suited for anything more than online gaming or voice communications. Others will produce a sound that is perfectly fine for audiobook recording.

Base-model condenser mics will cost around $200 to $250 for starters. Some cost as much as $4,000 or more! These mics tend to offer an, overall, less noisy sound quality than USB mics, but as you can see, the financial investment is a bit higher.

As mentioned, a pre-amp/interface is a box that connects the condenser mic with the computer. The mic plugs into the box with a standard, 3-pronged, XLR cable and a USB cable comes out of the box to go to the computer. As with microphones, the price range for these boxes can be wide. Budget around $100 to $150, but make sure you're not paying for features you don't need, or don't know how to use, and won't take the time to find out.

Let's Talk About My Equipment

Noah ~ *When I moved to my new apartment and had my booth installed, I was still using my USB Yeti mic. It sounded fine, but I had reached a point where I wanted to make my sound better, so I switched to a condenser mic. A condenser mic can't plug in directly to most computers, so I had to buy an interface. I got the Scarlet 2i2 and it worked great for a while. At some point, for reasons still unknown to me, my overall sound quality was not working, so I bought a mixer that included compression and a high-pass filter. That did the trick for a time, but then the computer I was using went kablooey, so I had to buy a new one, and at that point, my sound quality was not making me happy. I called my friend Gary, and he suggested taking the mixer out of the equation, since sometimes, the least amount of equipment between your voice and your computer, the better. Sure enough, that worked.*

The point of this is that your situation can change over time. Depending on your circumstances, you may need more or less equipment. But reviewing your setup and your sound periodically is a good thing to do.

There are two schools of thought on the use of headphones. There are some great narrators out there who don't use them. They feel they perform better without the sound of their voice amplified in their ears. Some have said a pitfall of headphones is that one could fall in love with the sound of one's voice, leading to overacting or a distracted performance.

The other school uses headphones. Headphones can provide intimacy and immediacy to the recording and acting process. Some narrators feel they put the actor in the middle of the scene in a more connected way. Generally speaking, if you're using "Punch and Roll," a method which helps you to be able to hear clearly where to come in.

Headphones are crucial during the editing process. Listening to your recording through external speakers may not allow you to hear all the extraneous noises, mouth sounds and little pops and crackles that need to be edited out of the final production.

The kind or brand of headphones you use is, again, a very subjective thing. It all comes down to ear and ear canal structure and the frequencies that resonate, both literally and figuratively. Plus, you'll need to find what feels comfortable on your head for long periods of time.

My Favorite Set of Headphones—A Love Story

Noah ~ For a long time, my favorite set of headphones were... I can't even remember the brand. It began with an "A." They cost $25. There was something about the clarity and the volume level *they provided that tickled me from my malleus to my metatarsals.*

The first set lasted about a year when one of the ear cups became dislodged from the whoopie-doo housing. Sorry for all the technical jargon. I immediately started scouring the Internet to find more of the headphones. I had to have them!

I wound up buying three or four sets. In the meantime, I did things like tie a bandana around the outside of the broken ones to secure them to my cranial structure—something I've seen Erin do, as well. Thankfully, audiobooks are not a visual medium. It wasn't a good look for me. Sadly, each of the subsequent sets of headphones broke in the same way after about three to four months' use. I had to let go of my obsession and move on. Life can be cruel like that.

Finding a new set was not easy. Once again, thank the heavens for easy return policies. I finally settled on a pair of Sennheisers. I tried ones that were more expensive and less, but for me, at least, there wasn't much difference between them. Here's hoping you can find a pair of $25 cans that rock your socks and don't break every four months.

Recording software, or a DAW (Digital Audio Workstation), is also a very subjective matter. Pro-Tools may be the "standard" software used in recording studios, but it's expensive and sometimes more complicated than other programs. Some studios use Reaper, but there are lots of options. The bells and whistles Pro-Tools or Reaper provide are pretty much useless when it comes to producing an audiobook.

Everyone has a different innate sense of order and definition of what feels intuitive to them. One person might think Pro-Tools is so intuitive it's ridiculous, while another could look at Pro-Tools and go, "Er... um... HUH?"

Don't let anybody tell you that you have to use any one certain tool. Experimentation and trial and error are key. Many paid programs offer a free trial of some kind. Yes, some programs can do more than others, but, for example, Audacity is a completely free, open-source recording program and thousands of audiobooks a year are produced using it.

Quick DAW McGraw

Noah ~ Erin cracks me up. First of all, she's hysterical. Not, like, you know...certifiable. I mean, like, really funny. She is always telling me how un-tech-savvy she is. I started out using a software program called Audacity. It felt very intuitive to me. Granted, I learned enough of how to use it to do my work, but its capabilities go much further.

Erin has used Audacity, Reaper, Studio One and maybe some others, as well. Her background includes working in audio description. She's had to use programs like Final Cut and Vegas Pro, working with both audio and video. Her ability to understand these programs, though she would tell you differently, humble one that she is, goes far beyond my own. She's schooled me on lots of things that have made me a better editor, like how to remove a mouth-pop from the middle of a word.

Eventually, I did move on to Studio One, which is also a great DAW (Pop quiz...what does that stand for?), though I still edit in Audacity because it's easier for me. I know Pro-Tools is a very popular program, but, for me, the cost and the learning curve aren't worth it. But I bet Erin could show you how to use it! (Pop quiz answer: Digital Audio Workstation)

Even with a modest budget, you can equip yourself with the tools you need to begin recording and editing audiobooks.

THE BUSINESS OF PUBLISHING

As an author, you have special considerations you need to assess regarding audiobook publication. Before diving in head first, it's important to figure out in which pool you'll be making a splash, and if you're even allowed to swim.

If you're a traditional or small press published author, it will be important to check your contract before beginning. Some publishers do not retain the rights to audio productions, and you can freely produce the audiobook as an indie project. Be sure to ask about things like use of cover art and other content, since many publishers maintain those rights, and owning publishing rights does not necessarily grant you permission to use all things associated with your publication.

If, after checking your contract, you discover you don't hold the rights to produce your books in audio, all is not lost. It never hurts to ask. Some publishers have no intention of publishing audiobooks and will grant those rights back to you simply for inquiring. Others may offer them as part of a negotiation for additional contracted books, while another publisher may be willing to facilitate the audiobook production themselves at your request. So exhaust all options before calling the medium a lost cause.

ACX Distribution

Owned by Amazon, ACX is an indie publishing exchange that facilitates the relationship between authors and narrators. With ACX, an author can publish exclusively for a 40% royalty rate, or publish non-exclusively at a lesser royalty rate of 25% for added flexibility and distribution channels.

Why choose to be exclusive with ACX?

- ▶ 40% royalty rate.
- ▶ Royalty Share contracts.
- ▶ Distribution to Amazon, Audible, and iTunes—the largest volume platforms.

Why choose to be nonexclusive?

- ▶ 25% royalty rate.
- ▶ Distribution to Amazon, Audible, and iTunes—the largest volume platforms.
- ▶ Not tied to ACX for distribution and can use other vendors to distribute the book.
- ▶ Only way to produce audiobooks in CD format while using ACX, since the exclusive channels only offer digital downloads.
- ▶ Ability to distribute audiobooks to library platforms.

Whether exclusive or nonexclusive, below items are the same:

- ▶ $50 Bounty.
- ▶ Seven-year contract term.
- ▶ 100% control over narrator or project selection.
- ▶ Currently only available to those with a US or UK bank account, tax ID or residence.

Publishing Options

Even though ACX is the most popular platform for indie authors and narrators, you also have the choice of trying to sell your audiobook publishing rights directly to Audible or one of the many other audio publishers such as MacMillan, Blackstone, Tantor, Gumroad, and Author's Republic—Audiobooks.com, among others.

Publishing contracts vary from publisher to publisher. If you're an author with low sales figures and/or one with no desire or drive to be a bestseller, this may be an attractive option, but if your sales are significant, some contracts could cost you in the long run. It never hurts to explore the possibilities and weigh options, but be careful to calculate the long-term impact this decision might have on your career in a growing industry, since some publishing contracts can be very limiting.

An additional thing to note when granting audio rights to a publisher is that you may have no control over who is chosen to narrate your book. If selecting the right narrator is important to you, this will be something to discuss with a prospective publisher before signing a contract. You can always request a specific narrator or narration team, and they may grant your request, but it's not guaranteed. Also, narrators who seek contracts with publishers will often not get a say in what they narrate. This lack of clear influence is an important consideration for both indie authors and narrators who want to have the freedom to conduct their business as they choose.

International Options
Non-ACX publishers may be a good way for Canadian and international authors outside of the US and UK to break into audiobooks. ACX is not available to them at this time unless they have a valid US or UK address, tax ID number, and bank account. ACX has pledged to expand their international presence, but as of yet, it is limited.

A Cornucopia of Characters

Erin ~ *Just a quick aside from the peanut gallery: I love having the opportunity to audition for the titles I choose. I get to try on all kinds of different characters and styles of writing. In that way, auditioning is fun. But there is something to be said for having a publisher give you a title. It stretches the acting muscles. For instance, I don't consider myself very good at accents, so I tend not to audition for books that require them. But sometimes titles are assigned to me with characters that clearly have accents. Hoo Boy. That takes some quick studying, frantic calls to Noah, and many, many retakes. Each time I complete a book that challenges me, I get better and more confident. I like having the control working on ACX affords me. Sometimes, however, fully submitting to someone else's control offers a real opportunity for growth (in case you didn't catch it—that was a wink to the Romance writers out there). With all that said, I love both the traditional path and the indie path through ACX.*

If, after considering your publishing rights, vision for success, and best distribution strategy, you decide on the indie path with ACX, it's time to figure out how best to pay for the production. It's important to understand financial limitations before requesting auditions. As with any business venture, setting expectations is a critical key to success.

Since this book focuses on indie audiobook publishing, we'll assume you'll be using ACX for the purpose of this and subsequent chapters. Because contractual terms and conditions will differ with other publishers, it's difficult to provide any guidance without knowing the details. ACX, which allows authors to choose their narrators and narrators to choose their projects, is the most popular way to publish indie audiobooks. It is, in our opinion, a well-organized, easy to navigate platform, with very few glitches and an excellent support staff. With that said, even if you choose to contract with a publisher, there are many topics in this book that can be helpful when communicating with publisher contacts, so the following information is useful whether you use ACX or not.

THE ECONOMICS OF AUDIOBOOKS

THERE ARE TWO BASIC OPTIONS FOR HOW AUDIOBOOK productions are funded/paid for—frontend and backend.

Frontend Contract

One way to pay for, or be paid for, an audiobook production is by Per Finished Hour (PFH) rate. This method allows an author to pay the entire cost at the completion of the audiobook production in a lump sum equal to the per hour rate multiplied by the finished hours of the audiobook, without any further obligation to the narrator. Authors keep all royalties earned from the audiobook.

Backend Contract

Another type of agreement is Royalty Share (RS). There are no upfront costs to the author, and the narrator assumes all production liabilities, but the 40% received in royalties are split 50/50 between the author and the narrator for seven years.

Hybrid Contract

This type of agreement is the same as the RS in essence, but it offers an additional PFH payment to help offset the narrator's production expenses.

It's important for you to understand what impact frontend versus backend contracting will have on the wallet, both now and in the future.

Per Finished Hour (PFH)

Let's say the book you want to produce or audition for is ten hours long, and the project contracted at $50 PFH. As we've detailed, it can take four hours or more to produce one hour of audio. While you will get $500 for that ten-hour finished product, that might represent, for example, forty hours of actual work at around $12.50 per hour. If you hire a post-production professional, at the cost of $75 PFH, you would save about twenty hours of time, but would end up $250 in the hole. Under these circumstances, doing your own editing and mastering would be necessary in order to not go broke.

One of the things we hope to achieve in writing this book is a greater level of understanding on the parts of both author and narrator for what their counterpart has on their plate when they decide to produce or narrate an audiobook.

Narrators understand that when an author looks at paying $225 or more PFH for an audiobook production, that's a lot of money—$2,250 for a ten-hour book, coming out of their pocket. We believe narrators appreciate and respect that indie authors want and are willing to put up their own money to pursue the creation of audiobooks. Let's face it, especially for those who do all or most of their narration work through ACX, without authors; there's nothing to record.

When authors appreciate how many hours it takes to produce an audiobook, as well as other costs the narrator may need to incur for post-production, equipment, and software, it gives them a good perspective on why narrators, especially career narrators, charge what they do.

If you're a narrator, you'll want to consider that tipping point where farming out your post-production work increases your bottom line. Using the example above, a narrator who hires a professional to do post-production work will earn more for the actual hours they've worked.

Self-Editing
$2,250 (Gross pay) / 40 hours (recording and post-production) = $56.25 per hour worked.

Outsource Editing

$2,250 (Gross pay) - $750 (editing costs) = $1,500.

$1,500 (Net pay) / 20 hours (recording time) = $75 per hour worked.

Those amounts are before taxes and any other expenses a narrator may incur, like health insurance. Authors, you can see how narrators who make a living performing audiobooks and can turn projects around quickly will be much more likely to seek out opportunities that fall into a price range that earns them a living wage. You'll need to decide what you can realistically afford, even if the $200 to $400 PFH range is where most of the experienced narrators will be looking.

You can keep production costs low by being mindful of your audiobook length. A 100,000-word book equates to approximately ten hours. If you pay $300 PFH, that's $3000. You'll need to determine if that fits your budget. Shorter works will result in fewer upfront costs, but if the book is below 50,000 words, you might be looking at potentially lower sales, as listeners may be less apt to spend a credit on credit-based platforms like Audible.com, or full retail price on a four to five-hour book. Length does not truly equate to quality, but consumers may factor that in when choosing their next listen.

For projects that have more than one narrator, the PFH cost may be higher. Weigh the extra cost of using this type of narration and decide if it's necessary for success.

Depending on your marketing plan, it may take some time to get the attention of audiobook listeners. Hopefully, the resources in this book will help close that gap, but they aren't magic. It is possible, especially based on genre, for it to take months, or even years, to earn out on a production.

Recently, some authors have had success using fundraising platforms to raise the production costs for PFH projects from their readerships. There are some genres where this isn't advisable, though, such as Romance, since fundraising book production costs is not something the industry embraces. However, in genres like horror, fantasy, and thrillers, fundraising has been done successfully with the right strategy.

If you're wondering how you could afford the production of your audiobook, and fundraising isn't your thing, there are other options.

Royalty Share (RS)

Royalty Share projects can be alluring. With their potential for long-term monthly income for both narrator and author, this may seem like a great option. Sometimes it is. A title that sells well can bring in a nice chunk of change every month for both partners. We've heard of narrators who pay their monthly household expenses from royalty payments alone. Some narrators, often those who are newer to audiobooks, are happy to take on RS projects to gain experience in the art form. More seasoned narrators might only accept an RS project after doing their due diligence on the author's sales and marketing/social media presence, etc. Considering the amount of time, effort, and money that goes into producing an audiobook, Royalty Share can be risky for a narrator.

If, as a narrator, you take a project for RS, you accept the risk that you could be working for free if the audiobook never sells or doesn't sell well. The risk compounds if a narrator pays a sound professional for post-production—editing, quality control, and mastering.

If you're an author who can't consider a PFH rate of any kind, Royalty Share will be the way to go, since there is no upfront investment.

Here are some things to consider before deciding to post for an RS contract:

▶ Are the author's ebooks selling well enough to entice a narrator to work on the project?
▶ Do both parties have a strong social media presence with a lot of followers/fans?
▶ Would a seven-year RS plan work if there isn't a solid partnership between the author and the narrator?
▶ Are both parties willing to split the 40% royalty rate, as well as any Bounties earned?
▶ Is there a high level of confidence that both parties will promote the audiobook enthusiastically?
▶ Have both parties considered potential costs in marketing the audiobook?

It's important to know there are many more projects listed on ACX for RS than PFH. The sheer number of RS projects could mean fewer auditions if you're an author, but if you're a narrator, it could mean less competition for titles, as there are more to choose from and many of the most experienced producers tend to favor projects that come with a PFH rate.

On the day we wrote this section, there were 1,941 titles listed on ACX. Here's the breakdown:

▶ Royalty Share:1,811
▶ $0 - $50 PFH: 52
▶ $50 - $100 PFH: 38
▶ $100 - $200 PFH: 25
▶ $200 - $400 PFH: 13
▶ $400 - $1000 PFH: 2

You can see how there could be more competition for narrators in the higher-end PFH rate projects, and arguably, fewer auditions for authors posting in RS.

For RS to work well, both parties need to be sales-driven. If one or both are not motivated, there's no real incentive, for either party, to take on the project. Marketing responsibilities should be shared equally. Make a list of tasks and programs to undertake and divide them up. Some you might do separately and some together.

Royalty Sharing is Caring... And Daring

Erin ~ In the past, when I have found myself without a PFH solo project or a stipend attached RS project, I have gone diving into the massive pool of RS projects—the thought being that working on something is better than not working.

My decisions about which titles to audition for have been informed by a variety of factors and I've learned some lessons— mostly that my reasons for choosing RS projects were flawed from a monetary perspective. I may have enjoyed the projects, but to be truthful, none of them have sold very well. One was a spirituality book that seemed to come just at a time when I felt I personally needed to hear the message contained in its pages. I'm glad I read it, but it has sold very few units. The other two were novellas written by a well-respected author. I had auditioned for full-length titles written by this author, and really liked the writing, but had not been chosen to produce the audiobooks. I thought that with this author's fan base and with how good the writing is, the books had a chance of doing well. They were great little projects that I enjoyed. What I didn't understand at the time was that Audible's system does not differentiate credit expenditures based on length of the work. Novellas cost the same as novels, and people are less likely to purchase them unless they are huge fans. The result? Many hours of work, little to no compensation.

Now, if I audition for straight RS, which I don't do very often, I do a tremendous amount of research including reading reviews of the book on Goodreads, Amazon, and book blogs. I go to an author's social media platforms and poke around. I check out the book's Amazon ranking. I look to see if they have other audiobooks and how those are selling. Even armed with this information, there is no guarantee that any title will sell well, or that any title won't. It's kind of like playing in Vegas. You can up your odds, but you can't be sure of the outcome.

Stipend

Fortunately, ACX created a program that can help to ease some of the risks associated with an RS project. Within two weeks after posting an RS project, ACX conducts an assessment to determine if the title qualifies for a stipend. Their rumored formula is based on a combination of book and ebook sales figures for the title, sales of other books by the author, sales in the genre, and some magical Audible earphone dust. ACX will email authors if their RS project qualifies. Authors can also check with support@acx.com. If a title does qualify, narrators must finish the book within a time limit set by ACX. When the narration is completed to the satisfaction of all terms set, ACX will pay the narrator $100 PFH in addition to the RS payments they earn.

A stipend payment can go toward covering a narrator's post-production expenses and can provide a small cushion as they work with an author to promote an audiobook. That ten-hour book would cost the author nothing to produce, but it would pay the narrator $1000. For a narrator who self-edits and engineers, that works out to approximately $25 per hour worked ($1,000 divided by 40 hours of work). A narrator who pays

$750 for post-production would earn $250 or $12.50 per hour worked. Unlike when hiring an editor for a straight PFH project could increase a narrator's pay per hours worked, in the case of stipends, performing your own post-production work may be more prudent.

Hybrid Contract

Another type of contract that allows shared royalties is a "hybrid deal." After listing a project on ACX for RS, the author agrees to share some of the narrator's production expenses with a supplemental PFH rate. The author pays this additional amount to the narrator outside of the ACX contract. The terms of each deal are negotiated between the author and the narrator directly. Hybrid arrangements allow narrators to pay for professional post-production services, while still accepting RS projects. Usually, it will cost the author between $50 and $150 PFH, in addition to the shared royalties.

It's important to remember that ACX does not support Hybrid deals through the ACX portal. Make sure everything is in writing using the ACX message/email system for consistency and the sake of both parties. ACX will most likely not intervene if there is a problem with anything that happens outside the contract drafted through the site. Most narrators who work under these contracts request a percentage payment upfront and then the balance when they upload the finished production. With these deals, open and honest communication is essential for success.

Self-Employment

Authors and narrators who have been doing their thing for a while know the pain and freedom of self-employment. If you're new to narrating, welcome to our world. As full-time, self-employed artists, we must constantly hustle to get the next project lined up.

It can take many auditions before for authors and narrators to match up, no matter the talent of the individuals. This vetting process may be why narrators who are in the highest demand always have a backlog of titles and may not be able to do projects right away and why top-selling authors may have many narrators wanting to work with them.

A dry spell can be devastating for any of us. Whether you are writing or performing, planning ahead by having a good workflow goes a long way to being able to pay the bills. Since there is no guarantee an audiobook will sell well, or a narration gig will fall into your lap, authors and narrators have to have a good strategic plan.

SAG/AFTRA

Under the Audible/ACX agreement with SAG/AFTRA (an actors' union), members must earn at least $225 PFH, or work on titles with stipends, for a project to qualify for pension contribution and health insurance eligibility. Union actors pay 13% off the top of what they earn for the pension contribution, as well as a 5% administrative fee to a "paymaster." With the ACX platform, the author sends funds to the paymaster, who pays the union and then the narrator.

For our ten-hour book example, using a PFH rate of $225, this would mean an additional expense of $292.50 for the narrator subtracted from the original $2,250 total payment from the author. In this scenario, a union narrator who does their own post work would earn $48.93 per hour of work and $60.37 if they farm out post-production, before taxes.

Fees and Additional Costs

Regardless of whether or not you've decided to pursue a PFH, RS or Hybrid contract there are some additional fees for which you may be responsible.

Authors will need a new cover sized to audiobook dimensions. Designers often charge additional fees to adapt your ebook cover. If you design your own covers, you need make sure you make the time to do so before your production is finished.

If you opt to have music as part of your audiobook production, there may be required licensing fees.

Authors could be charged an additional amount for edits that fall outside the narrator's responsibilities. Narrators are responsible for providing an error-free performance and high-quality recording, but are under no obligation to perform changes to the manuscript and may charge more to do so. These fees can add up, which is why it's important to have a well-edited manuscript before you begin.

Many narrators accept payment through PayPal. However, there may be a fee associated with using this method of payment, either to the author or the narrator depending on which option is selected. Some choose to use the "send money to friends and family options," thinking it will save them transaction fees. This option is only free if the person sending the money uses their bank account to send it. If they use a credit card to complete the transaction, there is a fee for the sender. Likewise, if a narrator sends an invoice for the amount of the production via PayPal, there is a fee from PayPal. Since, depending on the size of the payment, these charges can be substantial, it's important to figure them into your financial plan.

It isn't just narrators who have to think about the business side of the art. As authors, whose work to this point has been to write, edit, network, and market, you must now consider a whole new set of business-related challenges and opportunities you may never have thought of before.

As with any business, there are serious considerations to assess. Whether you're an author or a narrator, these financial, time-based, and physical resources will define what type of commitment you can make to your audiobook endeavor.

Royalties

The idea of audiobook royalties can look exciting if you're an author, especially compared to 35% of a $.99 ebook title or 70% of $2.99 at Amazon. Looks can be deceiving, however, because an author isn't going to see 40% off a $24.99 audiobook list price very often. It's very rare you'll see sales directly translate from the list price. Most are 40% of the Audible discounted price.

AL are Audible members who use a credit to buy books. Audible uses what they call an "allocation factor" to determine what the credit value is each month.

ALOP represents Audible members who bought the book without a credit, usually at a 30% discount. Royalties are calculated on the discounted price point.

With ALC, books were purchased without a discount or credit, usually through iTunes, but could also be Amazon sales, or Audible purchases from nonmembers.

The most frustrating thing of all is the lack of detailed reporting for royalties on the part of ACX. Authors and narrators can't see sales at the book level as authors can with other book distributors. Also, the ACX sales panel only updates once per day, and not always consistently. Plus, there is no transparency showing sales resulting from Whispersync downloads.

If a narrator does an RS project, they get a monthly report on sales of each title, and those sales are broken out into AL, ALOP, and ALC. They do not receive reports for PFH projects.

Whispersync

Whispersync is an offering by Amazon that allows the end user to move seamlessly back and forth between the ebook and audiobook versions of a title without losing their place. With a Whispersync title, Amazon adds the audio recording as a companion to the purchased ebook for a significantly reduced amount of money. Whereas an author might receive $3 - $6 per sale for their audiobook in the Audible or iTunes store, they may only make their royalty portion of the $1.99 Whispersync price. Amazon uses Whispersync as an incentive for new listeners to try their audiobooks, which can lead to other sales.

The downside of receiving this lower royalty rate occurs when an author runs a sale offering their ebook for either free or a reduced-price. Their audiobook is still available at the reduced price, even though they're receiving little or no revenue from the ebook. This could cause the author to not earn enough from the sale of the audiobook to cover the production costs in a reasonable amount of time. As an author, you have little choice about whether or not an ebook is added to Whispersync. ACX decides when a book becomes available for this feature without consulting the author or narrator. The only way an ebook will not become Whispersync available is if there is more than a 3% difference between the text read on the audio version of the book and what's written in the ebook version.

Receiving such a small amount of compensation for the audio version of the book may seem like a bad thing, but unless the ebook is priced as free, the author has already realized the royalties from an ebook sale. There is a reason authors price ebooks as loss leaders—discounting or setting the first book of a series to free in hopes that readers with buy the other books at full price. Whispersync works on a similar notion. Anything that increases readership will eventually increase sales, but you'll need to carefully consider this impact on your sales strategy.

Bounties

Bounties are another type of payment you can receive as part of your audio endeavor. If your audiobook is the first book a new subscriber downloads after signing up with Audible, you'll receive $50, provided the listener keeps the subscription at least three months. However, in the case where the author and the narrator are sharing royalties, each will receive $25. These can add up fast for an effectively marketed book.. Unlike Whispersync royalties, Bounties are clearly tracked on a separate report each month.

The bottom line is, simply, your bottom line. What can you afford?

For narrators, PFH is always the least risky option. As you build you backlist and word spreads, you'll be able to command a higher PFH rate. Conversely, RS on a strong-selling title will potentially bring you more income than PFH, for a longer period.

For authors with a bestseller vision, and the resources, PFH flat fee is most likely the best bet. Even if your first production takes a long time to earn out, you will eventually pass the threshold and the entire payout of royalties won't have to be split with the narrator for seven years or until the contract with the narrator expires.

Now that you understand the finances behind audiobook production, it's time to get started.

GETTING STARTED

TYPES OF NARRATION
SOLO NARRATION
DUAL NARRATION
DUET NARRATION
I CHALLENGE YOU TO A DUET
FULL-CAST NARRATION
AUTHOR NARRATION
WHY CHOOSE ONE WHEN YOU CAN HAVE TWO?

WELL-EDITED MANUSCRIPT
THE INTRICITE, CORNPLEXITIES OF THE FINLEY POINT'S
OF WRIGHTING, OR WHY YOU NEED AN EDITOR
I KNOW IT SAYS NIBBLES, BUT SHOULDN'T IT BE NIPPLES?

TRAINING
WHAT I DID BEFORE I DID WHAT I DO

SETTING UP A STUDIO
DID YOU HEAR THAT? WHAT THE HECK IS THAT?

TECHNICAL EXPERTISE

DEVILED SHMEGEGGE
HOW WAS MY ORGASM?

———

PSEUDONYMS

———

ACX PROFILE SETUP
THE SAMPLE CONUNDRUM

———

NOW THAT YOU'VE ANALYZED YOUR BEST FINANCIAL approach, it's time to make it all a reality—finding the best person to bring your words to life, or finding the author whose words roll off your tongue.

TYPES OF NARRATION
IF YOU'RE AN AUDIOBOOK FAN, YOU MAY ALREADY HAVE THE perfect narration in mind. Regardless, it's essential to know how you want your books to sound or which project you're best suited for when scouring ACX.

Not all narration styles are suited for all types of books, and unless you evaluate this closely, as an author, you may end up paying for narration that adds no value. Luckily, there are several different styles you can choose.

Solo Narration
Simply put, Solo Narration is the same actor narrating the entire book. This is the most popular style of narration.

If a book is written from the first person, female perspective, a female narrator will be best to convey the story. Likewise, using a male narrator is better if the book is written in first person, male perspective, although every rule out there has been successfully broken at some point. In first person POV, the narrator is typically the main character of the story. The narrator's voice will be that character, not their own. So having someone who fits the part is even more important. Having the narrator's gender match that of the primary POV character is not a hard and fast rule, but it is something listeners tend to prefer. Solo narrators also work on books written in the third person. In either case, as a solo artist, that narrator will perform all the voices for all of the characters, whether they are male or female, tree stump or dragon.

Dual Narration

Dual Narration can be a wise choice for stories that shift POVs between or within chapters. In this case, the female and male narrators will read all parts for both genders within their given POV sections or chapters. It is a good idea for the two actors to confer on how each of the main characters will sound, so there is some level of consistency between the two representations of the same characters.

Duet Narration

Duet Narration is a performance where the female actor reads the female lines, and the male actor reads the male lines. This style can be used for first or third person narrated books and adds an extra dimension to the story. It works best when the writing is crisp and free from excessive dialogue tags ("he said") that slow the flow. This style can be more expensive, as the PFH rate could be higher with two narrators working in tandem. It's important to make certain the way an author writes will make it worth the extra investment.

This type of performance can be used in first and third person stories. However, with third person, the Duet Narration team needs to pay particular attention to how they handle the transitions between characters and narrators, in order to maintain the screenplay-like feel of this style. Remember that you can open your audition to both Solo and Duet narrators and see what sounds best.

Duet Narration can and has been done with the two actors being in different locations. However, this requires an enormous amount of editing work, which could cost substantially more, and it may end up sounding like the narrators were not together while recording. Because of this, it's advisable to ask how the recording will be conducted, and if the narrators do not record together, sample other works performed by the narrators in this style.

I Challenge You to A Duet

Noah ~ Erin and I had been friends for about a year when she decided to leave her day job doing public relations for a local college to take on the full-time endeavor of the exciting, glamorous world of audiobook narration. She had been thinking about it for a while and was having her booth built when we met, so I knew she was serious.

I also had seen her act with her Shakespeare troupe, The Strange Bedfellows, so I knew she had some awesome acting chops and was so passionate about performing and the written word. On top of all that, I knew about her audio description business. I could tell she had her stuff together. I was excited she eventually decided to take the leap, full-time, into an art and business I loved, because I knew she'd be a perfect fit.

One day, I was perusing the titles accepting auditions on ACX and happened to come across something called Curing Doctor Vincent, by some writer named Renea Mason. This Renea Mason person had the audacity to be looking for "The Perfect Duo" to narrate her book. Can you imagine that? The project looked interesting, Renea presented herself professionally, and I thought, "Hmmm, I wonder if..."

The audition material was awesome, mostly dialogue between the two main characters and we had a great time recording it. So, after we hit "send" on our audition, we were giddy with anticipation to see if Renea would like it.

Like children on Christmas Morning, we waited with bated breath, checking my email every five minutes to see if she had responded. Damned if she didn't get back to us within an hour. We were totally charged up.

Working with Renea has been awesome. That our first Duet project with Renea went on to win an Audie, was such sweet icing on the cake. Erin and I have now narrated well over twenty books together, including Renea's Good Doctor Trilogy, her Symphony of Light series, Karen Amanda Hooper's Kindrily series and Cherise Sinclair's Shadowlands series. We love the Duet style—being able to work off each other and present an engaging, interactive experience for the listener. We hope more narrators produce this type of performance in the future.

Full-Cast Narration
In Full-Cast Narration, several actors play various roles in the book. There doesn't need to be a different actor for every character, as narrators can use different voices and accents, but this style goes beyond Duet Narration to include more and different voices.

For indie authors and narrators, this mode of production will probably be out of reach, unless the team has some pretty deep pockets and the means with which to record multiple voices at the same time.

Author Narration

Whether or not William Shatner can or should sing, he did. We are, by no means, suggesting that as an author, you can't narrate your own work. Many authors have been successful doing so, but those authors typically have a background in performance, whether it be as a comic, actor or something else theatrical. Otherwise, they tend to produce audiobooks not a whole lot of people want to hear. That old assumption about narration being just like reading a book aloud proves to be their undoing. A plethora of poorly self-narrated books has spurred a small contingent of readers who refuse to listen to books narrated by the author.

If you're an author moved to give voice to your own story, we suggest paying close attention to all the sections of this book that talk about becoming a narrator.

If a production will be Dual, Duet, or Full-Cast, it's important to understand that the ACX system is set up for an author to contract with one entity only. We say entity, rather than person, because there may be production companies with ACX profiles that offer a variety of services, including narration.

At the end of the process, the author will pay that producer. That individual or company will then be responsible for paying the various players.

For independent narrators engaging in multi-voice productions, where only one individual will contract with and be paid by the author, a separate agreement is needed between narrators. That's something the actors should discuss between each other before contracting a project.

Why Choose One When You Can Have Two?

Renea ~ I remember when I listened to my first Duet narrated book. I had started listening to a series that changed narrators, mid-stream, to one who is on my top-ten list of favorites. The first few books were good, the ones he narrated himself, were fantastic as always. However, in a later book, they added a female narrator to the mix. For the first few chapters, it was strange as I adjusted to the style, but by the end of the book, the dynamic and the heat created in each scene was incomparable. I was hooked.

I listened to every Duet narrated story I could find. I knew from the very moment Terri Berg had me sitting at my computer writing an audition call, Duet was the style I wanted. My books contain heavy dialogue, so I knew the method would be perfect. I tossed the request into the audition call, hoping just maybe, if I wished on enough stars, I might get something that was half as good as that first book that hooked me.

What I got was even better. I listened to Noah and Erin's audition three times, trying to make sure it was real before I casually sent it to Terri and said, "THIS. IS. IT!"

If you haven't listened to a Duet Narration, I suggest doing so as part of your due diligence.

WELL-EDITED MANUSCRIPT

A READY-TO-PRODUCE MANUSCRIPT IS FREE FROM TYPOS, character inconsistencies, punctuation issues, and incorrect grammar. Every author needs an editor. Many authors feel they can self-edit, but it takes an editor, someone outside the story, to polish the manuscript. The need for an editor may seem like a no brainer, but we can't tell you how many times we have heard about narrators receiving scripts that have been published as books but clearly not been properly edited. Why is this important? Some narrators will contact the author to ask questions if there is a typo or inconsistency, which adds time to the production process. Some will record exactly what's written and then charge for any fixes that require recording, which adds time and expense.

Even books contracted as RS may result in the narrator charging the author for extra recording time if they have to make substantial changes. If you think there's any chance you might want to make changes to your manuscript, wait until you're sure it's finished before trying to produce it as an audiobook. Be certain the manuscript sent to the narrator is the final. Otherwise, you can wind up wasting your own and the narrator's time with unedited work, unreasonable change requests, and unrealistic expectations. You could also risk generating a sour reputation in the industry. Maintaining respectful and reasonable expectations will make for a smoother process for both parties.

When evaluating your manuscript, assess whether it's a good fit for audio. If your book includes large passages of text messages that would not be easily understood in audio format, you may want to reconsider producing that book in audio format, or rewriting those sections to flow better, keeping in mind that the difference between the ebook and audiobook could make the book ineligible for Whispersync.

The Intricite, Cornplexities Of The Finley Point's Of Wrighting, or Why You Need An Editor

Renea ~ One thing I can say for sure is that I've never heard a bestselling author say, "I don't need an editor." Unfortunately, I have encountered many indie authors who feel editing is optional. A good editor is not optional if you're a professional writer. No, having Noah's cousin Ralphie proofread does not count.

In 2015, I published an anthology called Just Desserts featuring twenty-two different authors, all with original works. One of my requirements for acceptance into the publication was the manuscript had to be professionally edited. Several authors had to sit out because it was an investment they weren't willing to make. Unfortunately, this practice is what leads to the stigma surrounding indie publishing—that it's not as good as work published by the bigger publishing houses. In many cases, this isn't true, but those who don't see the value in a good editor prove the naysayers right every time.

You'll also notice that I say "a good editor." This distinction is important since editing and proofreading are not the same. A good editor will find the flaws in your work, call you on your bad habits, polish the text, and improve the overall readability of the work, which is a different skillset than proofreading. For example, when I submitted Curing Doctor Vincent to Nancy Cassidy, who also happens to be the editor of this book, she made it very clear I started the book in the wrong place, and while the story was OK, it wasn't great. With her guidance, I added two chapters to the beginning, a subplot which went on to weave throughout the trilogy, and a chapter toward the end that showed a key character change I had glossed over in the initial draft. It was her feedback that made the book a success. Her critical eye, copy edits, and proofreading added much value to the work.

I don't just rely on an editor; I have a team of twenty-five beta readers who help me too. They give me additional insights, feedback, and review my drafts—a task for which there should be a medal of honor. My manuscript drafts are truly dreadful. It's they who allow me to build a foundation. They each bring something different to the work. I have four phases to my beta

65

reading process. Round One readers take the work straight from my head in all of its unedited glory. Some love reading this early work, but it drives others crazy. I refine the manuscript based on their feedback before sending it to the editor. When I get the book back from the editor, I revise the novel based on her suggestions and then give it to the Round Two readers. These readers love to make wording suggestions and look for plot consistencies. Once I update based on their feedback, back it goes to the editor for copy edits. After I receive the document back and make the copy edits, it goes to Round Three. These readers want a somewhat polished story but with enough typos that they feel as though they are helping, and they do. Once they finish and I make the corrections, it's back to the editor for the final proofread. You'd think that would be all there was to it but nope! Round Four readers are those super-attention-to-detail folks. They go on a mission to find any last corrections. Before I publish the book, and after I make the Round Four corrections, I give it to Tammy Becraft, a beta reader who listens to every book of mine using text to speech, which always reveals errors missed by the proofreaders. After making the final corrections, it's time to publish. Even with an editing process this thorough, errors may still make it into the final publication.

I'm not saying you have to follow my methods. I am a little neurotic about editing, if you couldn't tell, so something far less extensive would likely do. I share this because audio will take your words and give them a whole new emphasis, and if something is wrong, it can't be glossed over.

Even with my editing process, I still had a couple of issues. The spelling of a secondary character's name changed from the first book to the last. Noah was gracious enough to correct the *pronunciation for me. Again, I don't think we've made more than a dozen changes across eight books during the review phase of the audiobook process. Many narrators will read exactly what's written on the page and keep going. Some will charge you additional money to correct any mistakes in the manuscript, so a book filled with errors could get very expensive.*

Trust me; there's nothing harder than listening to someone read your mistakes out loud. It's almost like displaying them on a neon sign. So, make sure you have a good editor before engaging someone to narrate your book.

I Know It SAYS Nibbles, But Shouldn't It Be Nipples?

Noah ~ *I think you're getting the message about how we feel regarding editors and proof/beta readers. If you could have seen the "marked up" copy of THIS book we got back from The Awesomes—Haven Cage and Rissa Blakeley, you would have had a very hardy chuckle. I know we didn't. Ha-ha. I fell into a comma coma. We had a LOT of things to fix.*

I once narrated a nonfiction political history book where there were: Longpassagesthathadnospacesbetweentheletters. Try staring at that for a while and see if your eyes don't go bonkers. And this was, ostensibly, a final copy, traditionally-published book. There is some assumed association between indie publishing and lower-quality-edited books. I think that's a bunch of crap. The percentage of traditionally-published books I have recorded with a chunky number of editing mistakes is just as high, if not higher, than indie-published books.

Erin and I have seen all manner of mistakes. Things along the order of, "Roxy slowly guided her slender fingers along Declan's thick, hard clock." And, NO, Roxy was NOT attempting to find out what time it was. So...

In the classic Woody Allen film, "Take the Money and Run," Woody's character, Virgil, attempts to rob a bank by giving the teller a handwritten note, which says, in part, "I'm pointing a gub at you." Virgil and the teller go back and forth, arguing as to whether the note says gun or gub. Erin and I get like that, at times, in the booth. While we can clearly tell whether it's an "n" or a "b" in print, sometimes we puzzle over whether the author meant to spell out nipples or nibbles.

You wonderful authors spend so much time crafting your story. Please invest the time and money to have someone who knows what they're doing read and edit your manuscript. It will be better for you, your readers, and for us when we perform your work.

Renea's right—steer clear of my cousin, Ralphie. He's a great guy—quick with numbers, but he stopped school after the fourth grade to be a "bag boy" for a local...um... construction company. He's not so good with, you know, English stuff.

TRAINING
NARRATORS WHO WISH TO ATTRACT AUTHORS TO THEIR work and to become better at their craft will need to train. There may be some individuals with a certain innate talent, but most need to learn how to act effectively for different types of performance environments. Although the basics of acting are always the same, the art of acting on camera is different from the art of acting on stage. Likewise, audiobook acting has its own unique components.

You can find classes to take in most major metropolitan areas. If you've never acted before, perhaps an "Acting 101" course would be a good place to start, but you'll also need to seek out voice acting and narration classes.

Thankfully, the Internet can offer some options for those unable to attend a class in person. You can do an online search for "audiobook narration classes." There are lots of tutorials posted on YouTube and there are voice acting coaches who work via Skype or similar video chat programs. If you can attend an in-person class, some of these will provide you with a polished, well-recorded demo at the end. This type of training is great to look for, as you will need a demo to get started and showcase what you uniquely bring to the table.

One word of caution. There are some "teachers" out there who are, perhaps, more interested in getting paid than in teaching a craft. If you're thinking about enrolling in a course, online or in person, do your research and try to find honest, unbiased reviews of the course and instructor. Check with more experienced narrators through one of the Facebook forums. Make sure the person teaching has actual, extensive professional experience in the field, either as a narrator or a director/producer. Compare costs of different classes and balance the price against what they offer. Unfortunately, actors, in their quest for work and success and all that may come with it, can be easy prey for a phony, would-be teacher who makes promises which they cannot deliver.

What I Did Before I Did What I Do

Erin ~ *Being an actor, I knew there was no way I could will myself into becoming an audiobook narrator or an audio describer. I knew that no one was going to "discover" me ordering my coffee at Starbucks. So I did what all actors do. I went looking for classes.*

In 2007, I had a very hard time finding reliable programs for either skill (narration or audio description) and I was leery, as most actors are, of being taken advantage of. I searched the Internet and got a few hits, but most were for general voice over work. I took a private voice over class with Lainie Cooke, a lovely woman who's a singer, working voice actor, and member of the board of directors of AFTRA. I reached out to my network on Facebook, asking if anyone knew someone who did training in either of those fields. Nothing.

I read everything I could get my hands on about audio description and began stalking anyone whose name was associated with the field on social media. Yes, "stalked," but no, not in a creepy way—more like used that old six degrees of separation thing. I found out that a woman whose children were in school with my kids knew someone who narrated audiobooks. I used both these avenues to reach out to people working in the field and asked if they would tutor me. I met with the friend of the other mom and struck up conversations with anyone who would talk to me about the work. I discovered that an old acting chum was a narrator, and she told me about Paul Alan Ruben, a Grammy Award-winning audiobook director and producer who sometimes taught classes in New York. I met Joel Snyder, who has been providing audio description since 1981 online. It took a few years, but I got myself into an audiobook class with Paul and an audio description class with Joel.

During the "stalking" years, I began volunteering. Every Saturday, I went to Learning Ally, then called "Recording for the Blind and Dyslexic," and learned how to "direct" and then how to read and record books for people with low/no vision and people who have reading disabilities. I found filmmakers and *content creators on YouTube and asked if they would allow me to audio describe their material. I continued to take classes and put together a makeshift studio, which allowed me to provide audio description for The Described and Captioned Media Program. I was on my way.*

I still take a class with Paul at least once a year and now train audio describers how to write and voice description for television and movies.

In the beginning, training gave me confidence and tools, like well-produced narration samples to utilize as I went forth. Now, training helps me hone my craft, connects me to other narrators, and shows me when I am in a rut and how much room I have for improvement.

SETTING UP A STUDIO

EARLIER, WE SPOKE ABOUT BUDGETING FOR EQUIPMENT and the importance of a quiet space in which to record. Now is the time to order that equipment and set it up. As a narrator, if going into a store to try out different equipment isn't possible, there are many reputable online resources from which to purchase what you need.

You'll want to load software, hang sound dampeners, and arrange and set up the computer as far from the mic as possible. Once all of the equipment is in place, it's time to arrange the mic so that it is comfortable to use and does a good job of picking up your voice, but doesn't block your view of your reading tablet too much. It's also a good idea to test everything and check the noise floor—the constant background noise of the studio picked up by the mic when no one is speaking. If the space is too loud, play around with barriers and sound deadening materials, like Auralex, to see what can be done to bring both the noise floor and the ambient sounds down.

For barriers, remember the heavier the material, the better it will block sound. Also, remember any hole, any space, any crack will allow sound to leak through. Creating an air space between the barrier and the wall of the "studio space" will also help to block the transmission of sound waves. If a booth or anything in the booth is touching an outside wall, low-frequency noise can be transmitted and picked up by the mic. Once the space is set up and working properly, you're ready to learn how to use it.

What the Heck IS That?

Noah ~ *Erin and I have been recording together in the same booth for a long time. At one point recently, out of nowhere, there seemed to be a "hum," like the sound of a damp finger moving around the rim of a crystal glass. It wasn't a constant sound, but one that would occur when emitting certain "frequencies" while performing a book. It drove us stark raving CRAZY!*

So, what did we do? First, we started wrapping the elbow-booms in towels and stuffing Auralex foam in between the metal gaps of the arm. I was convinced the sound was coming from the metal "springs" in the boom, which, after time and being moved back and forth, could loosen a little and become more susceptible to vibration. Smart, huh? Sounds like a great, scientific theory. No?

No. The theory was good. The reality was different. "Maybe it's your microphone," I said to Erin. "Let's replace it." I had a spare on hand, which is a good idea—having spare parts around if you can afford it. Sadly, that change did nothing to stop the problem.

After weeks of having to do a lot of stopping to re-record certain words that caused the sonic annoyance, we were just about ready to bang our heads on a wall. Erin took a break from the booth, screaming something about low-frequency dissonant abnormalities (yeah—I didn't get it, either). I was about to join her, but first had to throw away a dead battery from my mouse When I tossed it in the metal trash bin, sitting underneath the sit/stand desk, the clang produced and ensuing dissipation sounded an awful lot like the hum we'd been hearing while recording

Yup. It was the trash can. The bleepity-frucking trash can! Grrrrr.

So, needless to say, the can now lives OUTSIDE the booth and the problem no longer exists!

TECHNICAL EXPERTISE

WHEN LEARNING TO RECORD PROFESSIONAL-SOUNDING audio, you'll need to—you guessed it—take classes, or at the very least, watch some instructional videos. These are different from narration classes as they deal with the technical aspects of making a recording.

Many courses with limited scope can be found online. ACX also offers some instructional videos, but they only go so far. Finding a mentor who specializes in using a specific DAW (Digital Audio Workstation) and working with them a few times, even if only via programs like Skype, will save you a world of trouble.

Learning to self-direct is a tricky thing. How does a narrator both perform and follow along to make sure they don't miss or change words? How do they keep their ear open for inconsistencies in character voices? How do they watch for overacting as opposed to being in the moment and acting?

We hate to say it, but you will have to listen to yourself with a very critical ear. Quality control is essential—check what you've said against the manuscript to ensure your words match what the author has written. Judge whether the emotional content of the scene is appropriately performed, ensure you're not too loud or too soft, haven't made excessive breath sounds or mouth pops/clicks. It's a long list of which to keep track.

It takes practice. Lots of practice. Like any skill, once it's learned, and if it has been rehearsed and repeated a lot, it becomes much easier. In the beginning, you may want to listen to full chapters after you've finished recording them. As time goes on, you may feel confident spot-checking sections where there was potential for overacting, or scenes where there are multiple characters, to verify they're all easily identifiable in the conversation. Eventually, you'll hear when you "go off" and will be able to stop, go back, and start again.

 Deviled Shmegegge

Erin ~ *When I'm recording, I tend to let my director ears turn into the mean, judgmental devil who sits on my shoulder, criticizing every sound coming out of my mouth. This is especially true if the book is new or I'm feeling unsure about character choices I've made.*

One day, while reading a chapter with three men and five women speaking, I recorded and re-recorded a paragraph several times, allowing that nasty shoulder-percher to fill my head with all kinds of negative talk about my inability to get the voices right. I got so worked up. The voices all sounded horrible. I stumbled over the words 'the round-faced witch edged towards the woods' so many times, I ended up screaming in my booth. Not pretty.

Clearly, I was no longer in actor mode. A paragraph that should have taken less than a minute to record took much longer. Any actor will tell you when you start listening to yourself and judging, you take yourself right out of the moment. Your performance become stilted because you are no longer living the character but are, instead, outside listening to yourself.

Knock that devil off your shoulder. Your director is not a judge. Your director is there to keep you on track. It's a delicate balance but one that certainly bears discussing and thinking about.

 ### *How Was My Orgasm?*

Noah: *How was my orgasm? Was it too much?*

Erin: *Hmm—let's listen.*

"Marsha... MARSHA... I'm going to... I'm going to—"

"Oh, Declan, let it go, baby. Let it go."

"MARRRSHAAAA—HRRRMPHGRRRARRG ooooooooooohhh-hhh, oooooooooooohhhhhhhhhh, OHHHHHHHH!"

Pause...we consider.

Noah: *I sound horrible! I sound like a chimichanga stuffed inside an exploding burrito. I'm doing it again.*

Erin: *I don't know... I kinda liked it. How was my orgasm?*

Noah: *Hmm—let's listen.*

PSEUDONYMS
WHAT'S IN A NAME?

Before setting up your ACX profile, you'll need to decide if you want to use a pseudonym for some or all of your narration work.

Many authors use a nom de plume. Some narrators do as well, wanting to have separate "voice personas" for Romance/Erotica vs. other genres. If you can legally be paid under a pseudonym, you could even set up an ACX profile under that name. Otherwise, when contracting on a project, be sure to let your author-partner know which name you want to use for the credits.

We have heard some narrators say that traditional audiobook publishing houses or ones that produce Christian or Young Adult titles tend not to use actors who have voiced Erotica, but other industry veterans say there is no such standard. Before deciding to use a pseudonym, it's important to consider that fans of that persona may not realize you narrate under another name. Both partners could potentially lose crossover audience in this scenario. Not to mention maintaining two names, from a promotional standpoint, means double the work and some social media platforms require you to use your legal name or risk having your account disabled.

ACX PROFILE SETUP
ESTABLISHING A PROFESSIONAL PRESENCE ON ACX CAN BE
as simple as crafting a well-thought-out and comprehensive profile. Authors will sometimes search profiles for narrators who seem to fit the book they're looking to produce and may message narrators about auditioning. Authors can even use producer profiles to start the due diligence process before starting to listen to auditions.

A carefully developed and personalized narrator profile will help you stand out amidst a sea of others who may have much more experience than you. If you're new, you'll want to highlight collaborative strengths even if you've never produced an audiobook before.

An effective profile contains both information about you and samples of your work. Using recordings taken from audiobook training classes is one way to populate a profile, but you may also find passages in books that showcase your unique talents—accents, ease with scientific terms, broad vocal range, etc.

 ### *The Sample Conundrum*

Erin ~ *It's not always easy to find appropriate samples. Many newer narrators use recordings of posted auditions, and that's one way to do it. But I think if you are going to do that, it is a nice idea to shoot the author a note asking if they mind you doing it. I still have one sample on my profile that came from an audition, and I use it, with the author's permission, because the author loved my work even though she didn't cast me.*

Be sure to choose samples that are representative of works you could realistically be cast in. In other words, don't pick a paragraph from a biography of Tolstoy if you have a voice that sounds like Minnie Mouse. Finally, author attribution is always a nice, professional thing to do.

Samples need to meet ACX standards and sound professional—no background noise, no mouth noise, and consistent volume. Start with three or four samples and label them clearly. For instance, "First Person Narrative – SciFi/Fantasy," or "Nonfiction— Medical Research," or "Memoir—The Effects of Burping and Sneezing at the Same Time."

IT MAY ALSO BE HELPFUL TO LOOK THROUGH PROJECTS posted on ACX to see what genres appear most frequently. If 75% of the offerings are somewhere in the Romance category, it would be a good idea for you to have a Romance sample on your page.

Remember to play to your strengths, targeting samples but being mindful to show variety, too. A good rule of thumb is to include at least one first person narration, one third person narration, preferably with two character voices of different genders, and one nonfiction. Once you start securing contracts, use samples from your completed titles. Audio samples must be of the highest quality. Carefully chose clips that best represent your work, as they are your auditory business card.

Posting a photograph can introduce you as competent, approachable, and qualified. Actors who have professional headshots will want to use them for this purpose. Narrators without photographs can search the profiles of some of the better-known performers on ACX to get an idea of what a professional headshot looks like. Please, please don't use a blurry, candid picture from ten years ago. It doesn't send the message you want to send.

In the "About Me" section, you have the opportunity to shine. Of course, leading with experience is helpful, as is describing previous success. This section is also a place where unique talents and aptitudes can be featured. Follow with why an author should choose you. If you've never recorded a book, or even a poem, what have you done that makes you the best choice? Is collaboration a strength? Is attention to detail a personality trait? Are chocolate chip cookies made with vanilla pudding added to the batter a secret family recipe? That last may have nothing to do with audiobooks, but it does say something about who you are.

If you're light on audio credits, you may choose to list acting, radio, or public speaking credits. Listing classes or planned courses of study may prove useful and show a mapped path to attain more skill. It is important, however, to be truthful about employment history and education. As with any other professional resume, an honest and accurate profile is best. Truthfully, whether you're hired or not will mostly depend on your audition and whether the author feels your voice matches the piece. Very few authors will skip an audition because of a lack of experience detailed on a narrator's page.

You can still fill in the awards and recognition section even if you've yet to win an award for your work in audiobooks. How? If you've recorded titles and those titles have been reviewed, key snippets of those reviews can be posted. If you haven't recorded anything yet, but have received written recommendations from people with whom you've done business that speak to your dependability and integrity, you might want to post those.

In the next step of completing the profile, narrators have a decision to make, but it isn't one irrevocably set in stone. The looming, intimidating "Preferred Method of Payment" boxes aren't as scary as they appear. No matter which box you check on your ACX profile setup, you can always audition for any posted book. So, what should you choose as your preferred method of payment?

We've discussed the difference between RS and PFH work. Now you need to take that information and make a decision about how you want to present yourself. When your profile comes up, what do you want authors to see? When you search for titles, what do you want your default parameters to be? You can always change your mind at a later date, so only choose what you are honestly willing to accept. If you have no intention of accepting an RS project under any circumstance, leave the box blank. Even though you may choose to audition for any posted project, it is best to list the preferred PFH range on your profile.

THE AUDITION

SHOWCASING WORK
TRUTH IN ADVERTISING
BESTSELLERS
THE BROKE BESTSELLER
AMAZON RANKINGS
REVIEWS
AWARD WINNING
SOCIAL MEDIA FOLLOWING

AUDITION ETIQUETTE
FROM OVERWHELMED TO OVERJOYED

CHOOSING PROJECTS

CAREER OPTIONS

NUMBER OF AUDITIONS

THE RIGHT VOICE
THIRD TIME'S THE CHARMER

THE FIRST LISTEN
THE PETRIFIED FINGER

COMMON COMPLAINTS

REJECTION
BECAUSE ONCE IS NEVER ENOUGH
PUT YOUR BEST VOICE FORWARD

THE MOST SUCCESSFUL AUDITION REQUESTS CLEARLY STATE the authors' preferences for narration style and types of performance. The more information you can share at this stage, the better the chance of finding the right narrator quickly and efficiently.

SHOWCASING WORK
MAKING AN AUDITION REQUEST ATTRACTIVE TO POTEN-tial narrators is an important step many authors skip. This part of the process is especially important in RS contracts where there are more projects listed and fewer willing, experienced narrators. Promotion here functions pretty much the same way you promote yourself to readers. ACX has some useful help files on the subject, but with the popularity of audiobooks growing year-over-year, and competition to secure narrators becoming more intense, it's important to stay nimble and up on the latest promotion trends, ideas, and tools.

In responding to an audition or an audition request, narrators need to showcase their value. While you can't add clips other than the audition itself, you can list social media information, provide links to websites or reviews, and write short and thoughtful notes expressing your interest in the title. It's also important to add this information to your ACX profile.

Things you can include that will make your partner say, "I choose you."

- ▶ Awards.
- ▶ Bestseller status of your books or books you've narrated.
- ▶ Social media following.
- ▶ Review quotes.
- ▶ Short samples of your work on your website.
- ▶ High-quality samples/demos on your ACX profile page.
- ▶ A well-edited and engaging audition script and manuscript.
- ▶ A professional looking book cover.

TRUTH IN ADVERTISING

THE AUDITION IS MORE THAN A NARRATOR SUBMITTING A clip and an author picking a voice. Check each other out. You're going to be working together for at least a few weeks. Authors, look at a narrator's profile and online presence. Narrators, check out the author's other titles and online presence. It makes good business sense. This research is the first step in finding a comfortable, reliable, and profitable working relationship. Investigating potential partners can help authors discover skilled narrators who may be just starting out and help narrators to find authors who are just beginning what may become a very successful career.

There is also something to be said for finding someone whose work style and collaboration style meshes with yours. Having a look at how a potential partner chooses to present themselves, what kinds of attention they have received for their work, and what the buzz is about them may be a useful tool. Narrators who don't know the publishing industry well will need to know what to look for, and authors who think narration works the same way as publishing will need to understand that the audiobook world is a whole new kettle of fish.

Bestsellers
Unfortunately, titles like New York Times Bestseller or award-winning author do not accurately represent how an author's work may sell in any format, including audio. We know that sounds crazy, since the word bestselling is right there in plain sight, but over the past few years, there has been a strategy by indie authors to form boxset anthologies, price them at $.99, and drive the collection up the bestseller list. They rightfully earned the title, and it's an impressive feat, but it doesn't translate to a guaranteed solid financial picture. A book priced at $.99 on Amazon generates about $.35 for the author. Many authors earn their New York Times and USA Today Bestseller status by participating in an anthology with twenty other authors for a box set at the same $.99 price point. Even if they sell 50,000 copies, that's only $875 per author, before taxes. One can't always assume the financial impact of such titles, so use caution.

Likewise, it's nice to think that every narrator who voices titles for bestselling authors will have some reader crossover from one author to another, but that's not always the case. However, there are things you can do to see if a book is selling.

The Broke Bestseller
Renea ~ *I remember the first time one of my books hit a bestseller list on Amazon. I had a fellow writer who was enthusiastic about this particular milestone. The book was Impostors' Kiss, a 6000-word short story I had originally written as a blog post for a Scottish Historical Romance author. My hero, Cyril, from my*

paranormal series, Symphony of Light and Winter, is immortal. My colleague asked me to write a short story showing what Cyril was up to in seventeenth century Scotland. So, I did, but realized since my publisher has right-of-first-refusal built into my contract, anything I write regarding those characters during the contract term has to be submitted to them so they can decide whether or not they want to publish it. If they refuse, I'm free to do as I like, but if they want it, it's theirs. I never in a million years thought they'd want to publish it. My editor, Kyle, told me he'd never seen them publish a work so short.

Several months later, it released, and for the first few days, it was in the top twenty on several Amazon lists. My friend who was list-focused said, "Woohoo, now you're a bestseller! You can put that title on your books." The book sold exactly sixteen copies in the first two days at $.99. So, since Amazon pays my publisher 35% of $.99 and then my publisher keeps their portion, I made $2.21. Many authors feel it's perfectly acceptable to use that title because they made a list. I don't want to diminish the accomplishment. With more than 4 million books on Amazon, many authors never hit a list, so there is something to be said for it, but as you can see from my $2.21 bounty, bestseller does not equal lots of money.

Needless to say, I didn't adopt the bestseller title at that time and didn't start tossing it around until I hit number one in some serious cash generating categories, and stayed in top twenty for much longer than a few days.

Amazon Rankings

Amazon ranks can be used effectively to attract narrators to a project. If an ebook is selling well, put that out front in your audition request.

Narrators interested in auditioning for RS projects can check the author's Amazon rankings, and authors torn between choosing narrators can research the selling potential of narrators' catalogs by checking the audiobook edition ranks on Amazon, looking for bestselling titles in the same genres as the author's work.

At Amazon, the smaller the number, the higher the rank—one being the best. Remember, there are millions of books sold through the Amazon Marketplaces. An overall ranking around 80,000 means the author is selling approximately one to two books per day of that particular book. Look up their other books as well. These numbers do tend to fluctuate with book releases but are a decent indication of how well a book is selling. Older works typically have a higher number for their Amazon rank. Be mindful of advertised impressive-sounding ranking numbers. #10 in "Triple Sub-Genre" category of Cowgirl, Science Fiction, Love Triangles may not translate to the same number of sales as #1500 in general Science Fiction. Also, is the ranking for paid books or free ebooks? Free books are easy to give away, but the majority are never read.

A great resource to help you figure out how a particular book is selling is Kindlepreneur.com[1]. This neat little tool will calculate the approximate number of books an author is selling per day based on their Amazon rank.

Reviews
Narrators, if the audition material seems well written and interesting, don't let current sales figures dissuade you. One book can be a game changer. Check to see what people think of the author's work by looking at verified purchase reviews on Amazon. Not that other

---

1 https://kindlepreneur.com/amazon-kdp-sales-rank-calculator/

reviews aren't valid—verified simply means someone purchased the book from Amazon. Most authors get reviews through legitimate places that may show up as unverified, but some authors purchase reviews, making them a false indicator of talent or sales potential. Also, consider the number of reviews. The more, the better. Readers tend to review works they feel passionate about, and authors who generate emotional responses tend to become noticed.

Be aware that Kirkus, Romantic Times, Publishers Weekly, and other literary publications' reviews are available for purchase by indie authors. In the past, these types of publications only reviewed up-and-coming books, whereas now there is a trend to allow indie authors to buy reviews for several hundred dollars. So, simply being reviewed by one of these entities is not an indication of potential success, as it once was. Read the actual reviews and don't make assumptions. An undiscovered author may not have stellar sales figures but may be on the rise, if the number of their reviews is growing, and those reviews are glowing.

Likewise, we suggest as an author, you read the reviews of a potential narrator. Read all the reviews of titles that are most like your own. If the narrator seems to get a particular compliment from different review sources, that may be a good indication of areas of strength. Similarly, if a narrator receives reviews containing repetitious complaints, that may be an indication of an area of weakness.

Award Winning

Award-winning does not necessarily mean the author won an award in which the book was read and assessed on its merits. Many times these are social media awards that require the author to get people to vote for them. Winning these contests can be a good sign of a solid reader base, but isn't necessarily an economic driver. Contests like the

Audie Awards and those sponsored by writing guild chapters, like the Romance Writers of America, judge a book or audiobook on its merit alone. Regardless, if it's a voting contest or a judged book contest, the fact that the author participated is a sign of interest in their career success.

Key awards to look for in a narrator's portfolio include Earphone Awards, Golden Voice recognition, SOVAS awards, and Audie Awards. These awards cannot be purchased and have nothing to do with sales. Remember, as wonderful as it might be to receive recognition for one's work, lack of awards is not an indication of a lack of talent. There are really talented people putting out great work who are never acknowledged in this way.

Social Media Following
Does the author have a social media following? Does the narrator? Twitter, Facebook, Instagram, etc.? How many followers? Are they active on those platforms? Do they actively advertise? Do they engage with their audience or bombard them with ads? Most indie books and indie audiobooks are marketed on social media, so making sure a partner has a platform, and is actively engaging with potential customers, can make a big difference between a partnership that makes money and one that doesn't. Also, be careful of authors or narrators who post inflammatory things, as this is bound to alienate part of your potential audience.

Not one of these things clearly determines how successful an author or a narrator is or will be, but they are indications of career commitment. Data like this serves to give each partner further information and a glimpse of how each might proceed in the future.

AUDITION ETIQUETTE

BEING MINDFUL OF HOW YOU PROGRESS THROUGH THE audition process is good business for both authors and narrators. For example, if you're an author without the funds to pay for a project, don't request auditions unless you're willing to do an RS agreement. Trying to convince a partner to do an RS project when they thought they were auditioning for a PFH project is bad form.

It takes time to audition, so being respectful of narrator's investment of this resource is important. Keep audition scripts short, tight, and well edited; no more than ten minutes in length max, which is approximately 1500 words of the manuscript. Most authors will have a feel for the narrator in the first 500 to 750 words.

Authors will sometimes put up several chapters of a manuscript and ask the narrator to choose what to read. These long selections make the audition difficult for the narrator, as they can't anticipate what an author is looking for, and have to read all the material to decide what is the most appropriate audition piece. Best to make sure the selection contains dialogue and is a solid representation of your work.

It takes time to listen to auditions. As a narrator, make sure audition recordings are clean, edited, and mastered. Even if you don't get the contract, a high-quality audition says something about your work ethic and professionalism, which may lead to direct audition requests in the future.

As an author, clearly communicate what will define a successful performance for you. Narrators can't read your mind or see your vision unless you clearly explain the details. Be specific about genders you'll consider, the voices/accents you want, and narration style (Solo, Dual POV, Duet).

If you have questions for an author about the audition material, communicate as soon as possible using the ACX system. If you don't hear back, which may be the case sometimes, make the acting choice that feels right to you and fully commit to it.

If you have a particular narrator, or narrators, in mind, there is a method to reach out and let them know. Use the search box to find their ACX profile and send a note. If the communication is favorable, and both parties come to an agreement, it can save having to go through the audition process. It's still good to have your preferred narrator do an audition.

Even if you have a specific narrator in mind and you make them an offer directly, your project will still be open for auditions from the time you post it until the time the narrator accepts the offer. In this situation, indicate in the audition request that a narrator has already been selected for the project, so other narrators don't waste their time auditioning.

Narrators, read all of the comments on an audition page to avoid auditioning for books that already have a narrator. Submitting auditions for titles with a narrator already selected is frowned on by both authors, who can be inundated with useless auditions, and by the narrator community, who looks at such actions as potential poaching or lack of professionalism.

ACX does a wonderful job of guiding you through the project setup, so there's no need to rehash that here. The ACX help files are robust, and the interface is user friendly. It is important as an author to keep your audition open until you have finished negotiating with a potential narrator. Authors can receive hundreds of auditions, and it may be tempting to close the process just to stem the flow. If you choose to close auditions, the ACX system sends a notification to every narrator who auditioned and notifies them that they were not selected. This communication may be sent to narrators who are very much in the running. The system doesn't inform the author about the message.

From Overwhelmed to Overjoyed

Renea ~ *I was told by several authors' friends that when I posted* Curing Doctor Vincent *for auditions that I wouldn't get many. So, that's what I went in thinking. I didn't understand the impact posting a title for PFH vs. RS could have on how many auditions I'd receive. Those who gave me the advice had only posted RS projects. My audition call said I'd accept either RS or PFH.*

I requested Duet Narration. Actually, I called it Dual Narration, because at the time, I didn't understand there was a difference between the two styles. I knew it was unlikely I'd get any Duet auditions, since even though it's my favorite, it wasn't done very often, and because it required two narrators, I wasn't sure if I could afford it. I also now know not using the correct name for the style could have hampered my success in receiving the right auditions.

The first ten auditions came, and I was overwhelmed. All of them were so good, making it hard to choose, but none of them were the Duet Narration I wanted. Then the next ten, and then the next twenty, caused a bit of a meltdown on my part. I couldn't keep up, and distinguishing one voice from another was difficult.

I eventually narrowed my choices down to three. I wanted to let all the other narrators know to stop auditioning, but the site doesn't cover that in a clear way. ACX has this little button that says "stop auditions." So, I went in, pressed it, and sat down to decide who to choose.

Suddenly, I received a message from one narrator asking me why he wasn't selected and another asked for feedback about what he did wrong. I had no idea why they were asking this. I discovered when you "stop auditions," the system sends everyone who auditioned a message saying they weren't selected, including the narrators I was interested in.

So, I opened them back up, because I was a bit frazzled by the process and was honestly afraid to touch anything else for fear it might send another message behind the scenes. I messaged the three narrators I was interested in and explained my mishap.

But as fate would have it, opening up those auditions again led to why I'm here telling you this story. The very last audition I received was from Noah and Erin—the more-than-perfect Duet Narration I'd been dreaming of. And the rest is history, as they say.

CHOOSING PROJECTS

THE ACX WEBSITE CAN BE LIKE A CANDY STORE WITH SO many eye-catching RS covers begging to be your next project. If you're a narrator looking in the $200-$400 or the $400-$1,000 ranges, it can also look like a desert wasteland. Be aware of the date the audition was posted. While most projects have been recently added (within the last month or two), we've seen offerings that had been languishing for months. There are many reasons why a project may still be posted for auditions after a long while, but the important message is if you're prioritizing your workflow, it might be wise to put your time into more recent projects. In the end, which projects you choose to audition for will depend on whether you're looking to gain experience, build your catalog, break into new genres, dabble in a hobby, or earn a living.

Find auditions that look interesting to you and try them out. Try lots of different types of materials. Unless you are gifted beyond belief and have lady luck as one of your constant companions, you aren't likely to land all of your auditions. So, don't worry about it—experiment, have fun.

Keep in mind, some authors' writing will flow more smoothly off your tongue than others. This phenomenon doesn't mean those more challenging titles are off limits, but that some people's brains are wired to adapt more easily to one author's style as opposed to another. Being in this business, as either a narrator or an author, requires constant pushing the envelope, stretching comfort zones, abilities, and writing and performing difficult material. Part of being successful is the ongoing process of expanding your capabilities and learning to work well with new and different projects. Auditions are an exceptional way to learn more about yourself as a performer, about what types of material best suit your style.

You've learned there are pros and cons to listing or auditioning for RS or PFH title, but now you have to make the decision. Should you audition for PFH titles, and at what rate? Should you audition for RS projects, and what should you look for?

Contracting a book at a PFH rate is less risky for a narrator and potentially more lucrative for the author, once they've earned back what they spent on the production.

Royalty Share contracts can be attractive for authors who don't have the resources to pay for the production upfront, but can be risky for the narrator if the title does not sell. If audiobook production is a hobby, sales might not matter. If financial gain is an integral part of your success plan, RS will require a lot of work for the reward.

The indie author community has many authors with well-written books, but who lack the finances to commission a PFH production or invest in a solid marketing plan. Like with any other community, it also has amateur hobbyists and, worse, scammers.

Read and write audition requests carefully. There are red flags to watch out for as you comb through titles up for audition. One situation involves authors who require narrators to purchase the ebook to use as the manuscript instead of providing an electronic copy free of charge. If you see anything that looks like this listed on an audition page, move along. There is nothing to see here.

Another scenario to be aware of consists of "authors" putting up short RS projects they may or may not have the rights to, with no intention of trying to sell the title. Once the narrator completes the work, these scammers use the twenty-five free audiobook codes from Audible, which are supposed to be used for promotional purposes, for personal use or to sell on eBay. Yes, things like this happen. These people often take advantage of and prey on unseasoned narrators. They don't care about the quality of the book or the amount of time it took to produce. They are not looking for partners. To avoid falling for this type of scam, check with narrator Facebook groups before auditioning, read the author's reviews, and look at their Amazon ranking. Listen to audio samples from other books by the same author. If they sound like substandard productions, steer clear. They are most likely not legitimate.

Self-publishing has opened doors for authors who were overlooked by big house publishers because they didn't fit the mold. The downside of self-publishing is that it has become so easy. The market is flooded with indie authors, many of whom are very good and others, not so much. It is best summed up by a quote we once heard, "It used to be one author sold a million books, now there are a million authors selling one book each."

In any case, it is a good idea for a narrator to diversify projects by auditioning for some PFH titles and some vetted RS titles so that as you begin to get more work, you'll be paid upon completion for some and have royalties coming in for others.

Ultimately, after weighing all options, you'll need to decide which terms work best for you.

CAREER OPTIONS

DURING A RECENT SEARCH OF PROJECTS OPEN FOR AUDItions on ACX, 35% (both RS and PFH) were in the Romance and Erotica genres. This statistic is not surprising since according to the February 9th, 2014 episode of National Public Radio's *All Things Considered*, Romance novels are a 1.4-billion-dollar industry. If you're an indie narrator who finds the idea of performing Romance uncomfortable, you may want to find a way to overcome your hesitancy if you want consistent work. Beyond the abundance of work the Romance genre affords, the community consists of an exceptionally supportive group of authors and readers/listeners. That's not to say that other genres don't have an equally wonderful support network, but the Romance world is a generous and collaborative community with a pay-it-forward mindset.

As a narrator, it's best to find a few genres that mesh well with your style. If you're just starting out, the sheer variety may feel overwhelming and titles that sound like they'd be a good match may be few and far between. One way to explore genre and style is to head over to the "Titles Accepting Auditions" section and just take a look. Record yourself using the audition material from a few different genres and authors. Feel which ones seem to fit your voice best. You don't have to submit the recordings. The samples are just a way to try out different types of writing, different genres, and practice your skills. Once you've tried out a few pieces, and either submitted them or put them in the trash, you'll be able to narrow down your genre preferences.

Choosing whether or not to audition for specific genres can make a big difference to your portfolio and career as a narrator. If you limit yourself to auditions for new books on quantum physics, you may find you have fascinating conversations with the authors and may enjoy working with them, but you may not sell a huge number of audiobooks. Publishers Weekly produces an annual list of book sales by genre—a great way for authors and narrators alike to get a clear picture of how well a particular genre is doing.

With so many different types of Romance projects listed on ACX, it's important to understand that some are sweet, some more explicit and some may be akin to aural pornography. You'll need to be sure you're comfortable with the language involved. A lack of ease and comfort performing a particular type of work can lead to a less-than-believable performance. Some scenes may depict situations you would never partake of in real life, but regardless, the performance will need to sound authentic. Considering and defining your hard limits will save you time and discomfort by helping you to avoid works outside your comfort zone. List genres or type of material you are not willing to narrate on your ACX profile.

Narrators have varying degrees of comfort with different genres, heat levels, and violence. When authors post an audition request, it's important to make note if a book contains explicit, violent or potentially offensive material and of what nature. We have heard narrators tell stories about getting half way through a book, finding a scene with violence or sexual content so disturbing to them that they were unable to produce the project.

Just like with any other story, narrators will need to find actable emotions in erotic tales. Put yourself in the mindset of the characters, find the feelings, and read the scene in character. Talking dirty into a mic is not everyone's cup of tea, but some narrators have a knack for it. They don't overact the sex; they don't "perform" the scene the way *they* think it should sound. The best narrators of Erotica put themselves in the moment and act, always keeping in mind the intimacy of the medium. It's the only way to keep Erotica from sounding like bad porn.

NUMBER OF AUDITIONS

REMEMBER, EACH AUDITION IS A POTENTIAL JOB. AS A performer, it's unlikely to land every project you audition for, but it has happened. Some authors take longer than others to vet and respond to auditions, and a narrator may keep auditioning for other projects, even if an author has already cast them in their head.

Be mindful. You may keep auditioning and then suddenly find yourself the happy recipient of five book offers, all wanting finish dates around the same time. Remember every hour of finished audio can take more than four hours to produce. Carefully estimate how many jobs you can complete in a given period and audition accordingly. Thankfully, ACX affords narrators the opportunity to work with authors in determining due dates, so negotiating with the author is always an option.

Sometimes authors don't receive the number of auditions they thought they would. This lack of interest could be due to a variety of factors. Royalty Share only auditions could be harder to come by since there are many projects competing for a limited number of narrators who will audition for an unproven RS project. Also, Royalty Share, especially if your book is significantly long, will be less attractive to a large percentage of narrators. Likewise, even if the author offers PFH, the genre, script, audition call, narrator availability, and type of narration requested could limit the options. Believe it or not, the cover of a book can have an impact on the number of auditions. If the cover art is not high quality or the aspect ratio seems funky or if the font used is comic sans, narrators may skip over it looking for a more professionally presented package.

Conversely, you may find yourself inundated with auditions and have a difficult time selecting a partner for your audiobook journey. In this case, engage readers to help. Post auditions on a password-protected page on your website, give key readers the password and create a narration scoresheet, and then let them help decide. The most important thing is to make sure the narration is something you enjoy listening to, because you will listen to it more than anyone else, when reviewing and suggesting edits. It's magical to hear a great narrator bring your words to life.

THE RIGHT VOICE
ONCE YOU'VE CAREFULLY ASSESSED ALL THE AUDITIONS you've received and whittled your choices down to a few, it's time to consider some key points before making your final decision. You need to find the right voice and working style to meet your needs. From the start, setting a tone of open and clear communication is the best way to foster a solid relationship, whether it's for one audiobook or a long-term partnership.

None of the following topics are necessarily deal breakers, but strength or weakness in an area can help you choose between equally compelling performances, depending on what is important to you as an author in reaching your goals.

Is the narrator:

▶ Able to perform all of the voices/accents needed for the production? If they have an accent naturally, is that OK?
▶ Experienced in your niche or genre?
▶ Established with a backlist of titles or are they new?
▶ Active on social media with listeners in positive ways—website, Facebook page, and Twitter?
▶ Willing to market the book if engaged in an RS contract?
▶ Willing to do interviews and fan engagement even if in a PFH contract?
▶ A recipient of any awards for their work, such as an Audie, Earphones, VSOA, etc.?
▶ Someone who has a good reputation with other authors?
▶ Interested in producing a series or multiple titles in your backlist?
▶ Available to meet the timelines you need to meet your goals?

It's not unheard of to ask a narrator or even a few, if you are having a hard time choosing one, to do a "second-round" audition. You might send them a different, short section to record, to get a better sense of how you feel about your characters and the narrator's voice. Keep in mind a narrator may not want to put additional time into an audition. This lack of enthusiasm to continue the audition process is not, necessarily, a sign that they will be difficult to work with. As we've mentioned, crafting an audition takes time, and if the narrator is a busy one, they may not have the time for a second round. But that doesn't mean they won't do a great job with your production if you give it to them.

 Third Time's the Charmer
Noah ~ *In my first year as a narrator, when I discovered ACX, I auditioned for a thriller. I had just finished my first Audible*

contract and the next one wasn't starting for several weeks. The author wrote back and said he really liked my audition, but wanted to talk to me on the phone and have me do a second round. I had the time, so I said yes.

I spoke with him on several occasions. He's a television writer/ producer, and perhaps more into directing than other authors might be. I liked the book and really wanted the job, so I did not only a second round, but a third round as well, plus more telephone and email discussions, all before landing the gig.

At this point in my career, it would be harder for me to spend that much time on one audition, but if it were a project I really wanted to do, I'd find a way to make it work.

Beyond a narrator's backlist, it's also important to check their reviews, specifically, the reviews of works similar to yours in regards to genre, characters, accents, etc. Some narrators are better at some genres than others. Every narrator gets bad reviews, just like every writer does, so it's important to keep that in mind.

Some things to think about when reading unfavorable reviews:

- ▶ Is it constructive/useful information or is it nitpicky?
- ▶ Is the Reviewer sharing a subjective opinion or citing a technical flaw?
- ▶ Does the review reference the narration or the writing? Both?
- ▶ Has the reviewer made similar comments on other audiobooks?

THE FIRST LISTEN
FOR AN AUTHOR, HITTING PLAY FOR THE FIRST TIME CAN be an unnerving experience. It's one thing to know someone has read

your words, it's another to hear someone read them aloud. Nothing can quite prepare you for that first sentence.

It's rare for a narrator to match the vision in the author's head. Even with the best communication between author and narrator, it's rare someone will be a perfect match. Listen for actors that best convey the emotional elements of the book. Over time, you may come to find that if your narrator is talented, the characters you originally envisioned could morph in your mind to take on the mannerisms and inflections present in the performance. It's amazing the dimension a skilled actor can bring to your work.

Remember, every narrator has a warm-up time for the listener, and their audition is going to be the first thing you've listened to them perform. Go back and listen to the auditions you liked more than once. You may feel differently the second time around.

 ### *The Petrified Finger*

Renea ~ *I'm not exactly sure how long my finger hovered over the mouse button prepared to click "play," but it was at least a solid fifteen minutes. There's something about listening to someone read your words aloud for the first time. I was petrified, and I'm not one to scare easily.*

For the first few words, I sat cringing, almost embarrassed by the ordeal. Again, I write Erotic Romance; I don't get embarrassed by much. My reaction was puzzling, especially since I hear from readers all the time about my books. It's the intimacy of the medium and the fact that it's not commentary about my work, but my actual words flowing from someone else's lips. I can only imagine how authors who have their books made into movies feel.

As with anything, the more you listen, the easier it gets, and you'll start to appreciate and enjoy the performances. When you work with someone as talented as Noah and/or Erin, you begin to look forward to each performance. But even then, there are moments of trepidation.

Noah did a fabulous job giving voice to Xavier, Marco, and Sebastian in Curing Doctor Vincent. I'm 100% convinced that there isn't anyone who could give a better performance, but we Romance authors have special attachments with certain characters. Cyril, my hero from Symphony of Light and Winter, was the muse that caused me to write in the first place, and I needed him to be perfect. Even though I trusted Noah implicitly, this was Cyril. I wasn't certain Noah, or anyone on the planet for that matter, could meet my expectation for Cyril. I remember writing to him, expressing my concern and getting a short and confident reply, "Don't worry, I got this." Then I was twice as worried. I thought perhaps I didn't communicate my expectations clear enough. How could he possibly meet my expectations? Did he know I was expecting the voice of a perfect, immortal sex-god?

When I received The First Fifteen, I had a similar experience to my listen of that first audition, finger hovering, knot in my stomach, dry mouth. An ever-so-slight panic attack. Cyril doesn't speak much in chapter one, and when he does, he uses a fake American voice. It wasn't an accurate representation of things to come. When I finally heard the voice Noah picked for Cyril—perfection. It was as close to the way Cyril sounds in my head when I write him as you can get. I think that was the last time I doubted Noah. It helps when your narration team is in tune with your work. From the get-go, Erin portrayed Linden and Elaine exactly how I envisioned them without any coaching or guidance.

So, my point? Expect the audiobook vetting process to be some-what anxiety promoting, but have faith that it will all work out in the end.

COMMON COMPLAINTS

AUDIOBOOK AUDIENCES HAVE A LIST OF COMMON complaints about narration. These can serve as a good checklist for authors while they listen to auditions and make decisions about which narrators to cast. Narrators can glean insight into what might turn listeners off in a performance.

- ▶ Voice doesn't match the age of the main characters.
- ▶ Voice does not match the sex of the character telling the story narration—male performing a first person, female POV story or vice versa.
- ▶ High-pitched, nasally, whiny, or robotic voices.
- ▶ Characters all sound the same—no acting in story.
- ▶ Overzealous narration/overacting—sounds like cheerleading.
- ▶ Bad or silly accents.
- ▶ Overly breathy or sounding out of breath, huffing and puffing.
- ▶ Smacking lips.
- ▶ Mispronunciation of words or character name, especially throughout a series.
- ▶ Not using the same narrator for an entire series.
- ▶ Pacing that is too fast or too slow.
- ▶ Poor recording quality—too loud, too soft, static, unfamiliar sounds, background noise, too tinny or too brassy, glitchy editing.

Some of these items are easily addressed in post-production editing, while others are not. Authors should look for these issues in auditions and either exclude or discuss them with the narrator before signing a contract.

REJECTION

MANY ELEMENTS COME TO BEAR WHEN TRYING TO SELECT one or two people for a role dozens, if not hundreds, are vying to land. It's not always the best sounding voice, the best technique, or the best portfolio that lands the part. In many cases, the criteria are subjective and have absolutely no correlation to a person's ability as a narrator. A narrator may not be chosen because they don't sound like the characters in the author's mind.

If you're new to narration, try not to let rejections discourage you. Authors have different visions for different works. If you're not selected for a project that doesn't mean you won't be considered for others by the same author. Many authors use more than one narrator.

Because Once is Never Enough

Erin ~ Fun fact: If an audition listing hangs around uncast for too long, eventually the ACX system will purge it. When those purges happen, every person who auditioned gets the typical ACX rejection notice: "Regarding your ACX audition. Thank you for auditioning for BOOK. Unfortunately, you were not chosen to produce this book, but there are still plenty of audiobooks looking for the right producer." Happy little notice, isn't it?

However, if you have a bunch of auditions that have been hanging out in the ether for a while, you will get a bunch of notices. There have been days when I have received seven or more separate emails from ACX telling me I wasn't chosen. Over and over again. So much fun.

It's part of the biz to get rejections and getting one or two a week makes perfect sense. It doesn't send you spiraling into the doldrums. But getting ten in one day? Oooooff. That can feel like a punch to the gut.

One thing to avoid is contacting an author to ask why you didn't get the gig. Many may be gracious enough to tell you why, but others will find this unprofessional, and it could hurt your chances with other auditions and other authors.

Actors who have been active in film and television work know that after an audition they never hear back from a director, producer, or casting director telling them that they didn't get the role, unless they know them personally or hear via their agent. It just doesn't work that way. An actor would never contact a casting professional or director/producer to ask why they didn't get the part, or shouldn't, anyway. Auditioning for audiobooks is no different. Do your best audition and then move on to the next one.

Some authors are kind enough to respond to auditions with quick notes, thanking the narrator and saying they enjoyed the performance even if it wasn't the audition that eventually landed the project. These small gestures are very much appreciated by the narrator community. If you're a narrator and an author reaches out to you in this way, make a point to tell them how much it means to you—just a small gesture that can go a long way toward furthering collaboration in the audiobook world.

Put Your Best Voice Forward

Erin ~ Noah and I can tell you how hard we narrators work on auditions, in some ways harder than some of us do on our audiobooks, because we submit a finished recording—edited, mastered, quality controlled. That means we are not only prepping the piece and acting the piece but also doing the post-production on it. Those of us who use professional post-production services get to skip this nitpicky, time consuming, and difficult step in the actual production process. When I've gotten notes from authors saying that they loved my work, but my voice wasn't right for the project, I feel like I've done my job. I feel like my performance has been heard and appreciated, and it matters so much. It's icing on the cake when they say that they will keep me in mind for other projects. It's always good for your sanity and your wallet to line up your next project, but for a performer, there is nothing like applause.

NEGOTIATIONS

SHOULDA HAD THAT CONVERSATION FIRST
DEADLINES
IT'S ALL ABOUT THE DATES, 'BOUT
THE DATES, NO QUESTION

THE CONTRACT

DISCUSSIONS AIMED AT REACHING AN AGREEMENT CAN BE fraught with all kinds of places to trip up. An author wants to make the best audiobook possible but needs to stay within budget. A narrator desires to make the best audiobook possible but needs to earn a living.

Narrators post a range of PFH amounts that they will consider on their profiles. Authors need to list their projects with PFH ranges or as RS. So, if a narrator lists their amount required in the $200-$400 area, they will be willing to negotiate terms within that range. If an author has listed a book as RS only, it isn't prudent to try to talk them into paying $200-$400 PFH.

There is nothing wrong with a narrator asking for a little higher than they are willing to accept and an author proposing a bit less than they are willing to pay. Bargaining is in our genes, and it is a way to reach consensus. However, once a price is agreed upon by both partners, it should remain set, especially if an author is hoping to use the same narrator for a series of books. Narrators, be transparent with authors if you think you will need to raise rates down the line, for any reason. If you have any indication about how much those rates might increase, share the information. Newer narrators will often be willing to work on a first project at a lower PFH rate so the author can get a feel for the narrator's capabilities.

If an author plans to use the same narrator for multiple titles, it is important to discuss the possibility of price increases over time or whether a price can be locked in for all the titles. This way you can budget for a larger project. If a narrator is not able to give a price range for the long-term, it might be wise to consider narrators who have that ability. If you have books already published, whether as part of a series or standalone, you can set these projects up in ACX and send the offers to the narrator. If they are accepted, you are locked in at the agreed-upon price.

There is nothing wrong with re-negotiating additional projects as they come up, but pricing should stay as consistent as possible and communication should be as clear as can be.

Shoulda Had That Conversation First

Erin ~ I've had a few instances where my rates needed to be adjusted. One was when Noah and I began to narrate together. Because neither of us had done Duet Narration before, we hadn't thought about the pay structure, and we quoted a price that sounded sensible to us but wasn't reasoned out in a business sense. Noah was already making a certain amount PFH, and I needed to make enough to make the work pay for the number of hours I was putting in. In those days, Noah was working with an editor on his solo stuff, but I was not. The cost of hiring one for our Duet work, based on our initial rate, seemed prohibitive, so I did the post-production work on our early titles.

Once we did a couple of books, it became clear our pricing structure was not workable. This added cost is probably one of the reasons more Dual Narration books are put out than Duet Narration books. With Dual Narration, the narrators are only paid for their part. In Duet, both narrators are paid for the whole piece since they both perform the entire book. So we spoke to our authors and raised our rates. A note of caution here: Authors can feel taken advantage of if the communication is not clear from the get-go. Since we were new to this, we didn't have the discussion we should have had about not knowing where our rates might end up. This oversight caused ill will that could have been avoided.

Sometime later, I got the chance to join the union! Joining the union is not just a professional stamp of approval, it also allows for a performer to qualify for union benefits, which meant I could afford to buy health insurance for my family and pay into a pension fund. It also required that I earn the SAG/AFTRA rate for any projects to be counted toward my eligibility, which raised my solo rate and our Duet rates yet again. We knew this could be a deal breaker for some authors. One author I do solo work with told me she absolutely could not continue to work with me, but then (and for this, I am so grateful), came back to me a month later and said she had worked it out. I'm pretty sure some of my authors felt taken advantage of, like I had pulled a bait and switch and I feel terrible about that. It has been a hard lesson to learn, but one I share because I'd like to help others avoid the kind of damage to personal and professional relationships that can occur without explicit communication.

Deadlines

The publishing industry survives on deadlines. Whether it is editing submissions, release dates, or marketing campaigns, getting work done on time can make the difference between a successful or failed book launch. For an author, the difference between releasing a book in July versus June could mean thousands of dollars in lost sales.

As the saying goes, "Time is Money." If you're a narrator who has received a contract offer from an author, before agreeing, be clear about your workflow and how a new production will fit into your schedule. Authors must be clear about any hard deadlines. If the author is flexible about the release date or feels you're the perfect fit for their project, they may be willing to wait till you're available. But an author may also have a launch plan that requires the audiobook be completed by a very specific date; in this case, they may need to seek another narrator who can work within the required parameters.

It's All About the Dates, 'Bout The Dates, No Question
Renea ~ *Since I started focusing on audiobook productions, I joined many audiobook Facebook groups and indie author support groups. Also, since winning an Audie, authors often reach out to me for audiobook advice. The number one reason authors vocalize dissatisfaction with their narrators? Missed deadlines. Not a week goes by where I don't see a post or receive a private message about author frustration for missed audiobook production deadlines, most wanting to figure out how to cancel their contracts.*

Since Noah, Erin, and I are a team, I've gleaned some valuable insight, not only from our conversations but from working on this book. Narrators are in a tough situation; they need to book work to pay the bills, and that includes booking work that will fill in for canceled work and the possibility that other projects may not be available. When you consider things like a bad cold can keep you from working for days or even weeks, it's easy to get behind schedule. Also, since the work is exhausting, and the voice can only hold out for so long, it's often difficult to make up lost recording hours. I tell you this because of the assumption, usually on the author's part, is that the narrator doesn't care. Apathy could be the cause in some cases, but certainly not most, I'm sure.

Pushed dates can be tough to accept as an author when deadlines are so important. My publisher missed my release date. I spent considerable money advertising the date and had a launch party planned at Barnes and Noble but had no book. The miss caused the launch to occur in a slower sales month. They reimbursed me the advertising costs, but the hits to my reputation, the embarrassment of the missed launch, and the potential lost sales were something I had to accept. I tell you this to show that authors are caught in a difficult place too. To market their book effectively, they need to know when it's going to release, and missing a release date can cause considerable expense, not to mention the numerous complaints from readers they have to answer. Readers have high expectations when it comes to release dates. In fact, this has been so daunting for me, I usually pick a target so far out I know I can make and then release it early as a pleasant surprise to avoid the complaints or don't tell readers the book is releasing at all. This lack of strategy isn't the best approach, since I suffer a significant number of lost sales, but for me, that's better than not keeping my word. I'm tremendously happy the anticipation of my work causes such a passionate response, but it's a lot of added stress if everything doesn't go as planned.

So there are challenges on both sides. The one glaring thing in all of these scenarios, when things go wrong because of missed deadlines, is the lack of communication on both sides. Authors should be careful to set reasonable timelines and build in some wiggle room, knowing that things may come up and your narrator can't exactly ask someone else to do their job. Narrators—speak up at the first sign of trouble, the more lead time, the better. Hopefully, these two things will lead to fewer missed deadline posts in Facebook groups where all can see turmoil.

THE CONTRACT
"I want to work with you!"

"And I want to work with you!"

THERE'S A FEELING OF EXCITEMENT THAT COMES OVER YOU when you see a vision begin to come to fruition. Since the world of audiobook production is as much a business as it is an art, we have to table our excitement long enough to dot our "I's" and cross our "T's."

The contract is, in a sense, a formality. It's necessary for work to move forward. The wording of the ACX contract is, of course, important, but the bonding of the two parties in the agreement is what makes each contract unique. Communication and attention to detail are vital to the health of the entire process. The contract is no exception.

ACX puts control of adherence to the contract into the author's and narrator's hands. For example, when an author makes an offer to a prospective narrator, they will set two critical dates that are then embedded in the contract:

1. Due date of The First Fifteen Minutes of recording.
2. Due date of the final audiobook.

Critical is perhaps the wrong word. Why? Because ACX is not moni-toring these dates. It is up to the contract participants to decide to keep the dates or not. If an author sets a First Fifteen Minutes of recording completion date of January 30th and the narrator says, "But I can't have it finished until February 2nd," it only becomes a problem if the author needs The First Fifteen by the set date. Sometimes authors will put in dates simply because they have to make an offer. Other times, the dates will be specific to an author's timeline for release and marketing. If this is the case, be sure to factor ACX's projected ten to fourteen business-day review into your timeline. Both parties need to understand whether to include it in the timeline or not, so an accurate date can be established when setting up the contract.

There aren't many circumstances under which an author can cancel a contract without agreement from the narrator. While we cover this in more depth at the end of the book, two of them are:

1. Due date of The First Fifteen is missed...and they're pissed.
2. Due date of the final audiobook is missed...and they're really pissed.

These two dates are crucial to the production schedule.

Now that all the contract mumbo jumbo is out of the way, let's go have some real fun!

COLLABORATION

COLLABORATION STYLE
THE UNDEAD AUTHOR

BOUNDARIES
CAN I BORROW YOUR CLIFFSNOTES?

BY NATURE, AUTHORS ARE OBSERVANT, CURIOUS, detail-oriented people. Their attention to subtleties, finer points, and constant inquiry can make for masterful storytelling, but when they aren't weaving words into fantastic adventures, their nature remains the same. They thirst for answers, need to understand the process, and will exercise their creativity in the face of uncertainty. Successful indie authors are also tenacious businesspeople.

Narrators are, in many ways, much like authors—emotionally and intellectually. Observation, attention to detail, and a hunger for understanding all make an actor better at their craft, satisfying strong needs in their souls. An important distinction between the two groups is that authors are accustomed to directing; they tell every character in their books what to do, whereas actors are accustomed to receiving direction.

You both have to be business-minded to pursue your craft, and prepared to take on some significant challenges. Authors are always driving sales, building fan bases and marketing strategies, while successful, working actors have to brand their product (themselves), audition many times a week, and deliberately define and manage their resources. Each has to be detail-focused to maintain a sustainable career.

There are some important similarities that, if understood by both sides of the equation, can create great collaborations. If a narrator recognizes more about what an author is up against in not only releasing an audiobook, but a successful audiobook, and the author comprehends all the steps a narrator has to go through to create an audiobook, they construct a solid relationship built on a foundation of empathy. This understanding goes a long way toward fostering partnership.

As with any successful business venture, understanding what is expected is vital. When all parties understand their roles and responsibilities, it leaves little room for misunderstanding and builds a solid base for an excellent business relationship.

To accommodate common needs for each project, narrators can create a standard checklist to share with authors when the contract is accepted. This organizational tool can ease your workload by limiting their inquiries. If carefully done, the checklist can serve as an FAQ, explaining why certain details are necessary, the best method to communicate, where to submit the manuscript, and preferred ways to engage on social media.

COLLABORATION STYLE
AUTHORS, LIKE NARRATORS, ARE ALL DIFFERENT. Depending on the situation, the desire for hands-on involvement in the production and post-production process may vary.

If an author has sold the audio rights to Audible or another publisher, the narrator contracts with a publisher. Your contact with and connection to the narrator will probably be much less extensive. You, the author, might collaborate with the narrator on character voices, but there won't be an ongoing review of chapter recordings. That said, many authors going through this channel choose to have little or no involvement, but the ones that do usually appreciate being a part of the process.

Some indie authors allow their assistant to handle all of the audiobook production issues and regard audiobook creation as nothing more than another revenue stream. In this case, as a narrator, you may never speak directly with the author. Others may require their narrator to do what they agreed, but limit communication to important business decisions and when the deal is done, so is the relationship, unless there is a subsequent project. Still, other authors may want to establish a lifelong partnership where they rope you into writing audiobook self-help books and other crazy projects.

Depending on what type of contract is signed, both authors and narrators may desire to have the other participate in promoting the title. The key to productive collaboration here is to set very clear expectations around how much time and what kind of resources each is willing to commit.

 The Undead Author

Noah ~ *In 2015, as part of a larger contract, Audible gave me a series to record. I was not provided a contact email for the author, but rather, the publisher's telephone number.*

I called and spoke with a very nice woman, whom I believe was an assistant of some kind. I introduced myself as the narrator of the series, asking if they had any questions and if they had any character information they wanted to share or accents/voices to request. I mentioned that I didn't have an email for the author, but perhaps they would reach out to them on my behalf.

Nice woman said that she would pass along my information/ questions to the author's editor. A little while later, she called me back, sounding a little uncomfortable (but still pleasant), saying the editor told her that, unfortunately, the author had passed away. The editor didn't have any information to share or requests to make because they weren't that familiar with the series. I was thanked for the contact and wished all the best.

I can't say exactly why, but something was scratching at my brain here. For whatever reason, I just didn't believe the author was dead. It took me all of about five minutes to find out that, not only was the author NOT dead, but the author was a husband and wife team who used a single, male nom de plume. They were alive and well and living in the Philadelphia area.

So, I made contact with the authors. They are a lovely couple, and we all had a good laugh about the rumors of their death being greatly exaggerated.

What's the lesson here? Authors—stay in touch with your publishing companies. Cards, flowers, singing telegrams. Let them know you're not dead.

You will need to determine how much interaction, discussion, and direction your partner is comfortable with. If in the future one person presses for more from the relationship than the other is comfortable, a simple reminder of the expectations you both set in the beginning should bring things back in line.

With all of the expectations set and consensus reached on how to proceed, it's time for you and your newly found business partner to start your audiobook journey.

BOUNDARIES

As we mentioned earlier, authors can be intense individuals and clear boundaries about communication will keep them from texting you at three AM when they're on their third pot of coffee, writing the ten thousandth word for the day, and suddenly remember they forgot to send the pronunciation for the imaginary catfish in chapter four. "The fish's name is VWARLDO, but it's pronounced Declan!"

Can I Borrow Your CliffsNotes?

Noah ~ *I love authors. I truly do. Their scope of imagination, story plotting, and character development—it's awesome. Sometimes they can be, well, you know, a bit verbose. I'm not talking about the books they write.*

As we've mentioned earlier, when I and/or Erin start a project, we ask the author for character information and a pronunciation guide. I will sometimes ask about a character's place of origin and their emotional disposition. This information can help me when crafting their voice. Most authors just give me the short answer: "Declan is originally from Belfast, Ireland. He came from a stable, happy, middle-class family. But when his pet goldfish, Renfield, died at a young age, Declan turned to the dark side and had been a brooding, caustic man ever since. That is, until he met Barney."

OK—pretty straightforward. He's Irish, has a chip on his shoulder, and is into large, purple dinosaurs.

Some authors, bless their hearts, want to give a lot more

information. A background of the socio-economic struggles of Declan's clan, the history of goldfish life spans, a compendium of data discoursing the effects of the color purple on the psychological manifestations of middle-class depressives. Pages and pages and pages of information that, while interesting, don't help in terms of trying to figure out if Declan would say, "mum" or "mom."

So, my dear author friends, when getting started on a new audiobook project, follow that golden rule: Keep It Simple. Save yourself and your narrator some time and stick to the basics. If the narrator needs more information, don't worry, they'll ask. And my narrator brethren—be specific and clear about what information you want—and be gentle in communicating what you don't.

As with any collaborative project where both parties are artistically vulnerable, there is a non-romantic intimacy to the process. Every author loves to have their work read. It's what fuels them. Narrators will not only be reading their work aloud for the world to hear, but giving life and breath to the author's characters. That alone can form an intense connection between the two. That bond can be healthy and lead to a long-lasting partnership, or it can be unhealthy and lead down a path that may affect business, so it's important to set clear boundaries. If narrators and authors do end up developing a more meaningful relationship with their counterpart, they need to create a safe place and way to discuss business concerns. In business, if you're someone who typically has a track record of failed personal relationships, it's probably best not to blend the two. Protect your business, and most importantly, your repeat business by keeping it all business.

Boundaries do not only apply when discussing author/narrator relationships. There is a third party in this business relationship, the listener.

Just like authors, readers love to hear their favorite books read aloud. Some readers become fans of narrators, and this can be exciting. Even though most won't listen to a book for the narration alone, there is a small but mighty contingent of fans who will follow a narrator from book to book. Remember that some in the audience may also feel a type of intimacy from the narrator's performance, just as they do when they connect with an author's words. It's true you will gain some listeners from your work alone, but most will discover you because of the efforts, time, and financial investment made by your authors unless you are investing heavily in your own marketing strategy.

Authors spend tens of thousands of dollars on advertising, and countless hours of their life communicating, engaging, and building relationships with readers. Readers are the author's most prized, cherished, and valuable asset. Gaining readers requires a tremendous investment and is vital for the future success of the author, so it's important that readers/listeners be treated with utmost respect. Narrators should always remember to engage with fans in a professional manner. We all like praise and attention, but keep things on a non-intimate level. Issues of entanglement can come up even more frequently in the Romance/ Erotica world. Be smart and be safe. As stated before, some attachments are not always healthy, and if a relationship ends badly for the narrator, that reader/listener is no longer likely to purchase a book narrated by you from the author. As with business partners, setting boundaries with listeners can also save a lot of headaches.

When narrators and authors click and have clearly defined and respectful boundaries, the synergies between the two roles can provide great opportunities and exciting business ventures.

PRODUCTION

PRE-PRODUCTION
IT'S PRONOUNCED, "SHA-DAY."
MANUSCRIPT PREP
CHARACTER VOICES
TURDUCKEN
DID I GET ANY ON YA?

PRODUCTION
TECHNICAL SPECIFICATIONS
I'M SORRY, CAN YOU SAY THAT IN ENGLISH?
ENGINEERING REQUIREMENTS
ENHANCED EXPERIENCE
INDUSTRY STANDARDS
YOU DON'T HAVE TO BE A ROCKET SCIENTIST
PERFORMANCE TECHNIQUES
SOUND EFFECTS AND MUSIC

THE FIRST FIFTEEN (TFF)
AUTHORS' RIGHTS OF APPROVAL
AUTONOMOUS PRODUCTION STYLE
COLLABORATIVE PRODUCTION STYLE
WHO'S RUNNING THIS SHOW?
MANUSCRIPT FLAWS

EXQUISITE

REASONABLE EDITS

REALLY? AGAIN? I TOLD YOU, IT'S PRONOUNCED "SHA-DAY"!

_____

FROM RECORDING TO COMPLETION

_____

FROM COMPLETION TO RETAIL

_____

You're on your way, but before you can get started, you need to make sure you give your business partner everything they need to succeed.

PRE-PRODUCTION

AUTHORS, PROVIDE YOUR NARRATOR WITH A LIST OF words—names, places, etc.—that may have an unusual pronunciation, including your name, if you pronounce it in a non-standard way. Sometimes the best way to communicate this information is via a voice memo. It helps speed up the process and ensures accuracy.

It's Pronounced, "Sha-DAY."
Erin ~ When Noah and I started working with Renea, we all decided to do an interview for her reader group, The Mad Masons. The idea was that they would write to Renea with questions for Noah and me, we would voice our answers to them, then upload the audio file for their listening "pleasure." Noah and I got settled into the booth, he with his glass of vodka and me with my multiple glasses of wine, and we began.

We had never spoken to Renea, but already adored her through the email correspondence we had been having with her. So, in the interview we thanked Renee-ah. We talked about how much we loved Renee-ah's work. We shared how much fun we were having with Renee-ah. After we completed the interview, we sent it to Renea to listen to. She giggled as she told us she pronounces her name like Renee. We never thought to ask. She was gracious, as she always is, and we added a creative introduction to explain the different pronunciation. But you can see how this might have caused a major issue with a different author.

Narrators, always make sure you know how to pronounce something before you record it. Authors, if you know you have a word, character, or name that is typically mispronounced, make sure your narrator knows how you'd like it said.

To help narrators find just the right voice for your characters, it's also useful to provide a list of character descriptions, including physical attributes and personality quirks, noting the ones you're particular about and others that are more flexible.

Both parties need to agree on where and how to upload files, either individually or all at once, for review on ACX, or DropBox, etc. Understanding how notes and edits will be delivered to each other and how errors will be handled—100% text accuracy vs. no problem as long as the meaning of the sentence is not changed, and keeping Whispersync requirements in mind, will make for a smoother process.

A good practice for narrators when receiving edits from authors is to ask them to include the incorrect line, the corrected text or note accompanied by the audio file timestamp, and a corresponding page in the PDF.

The last thing is to make sure you ask any and all questions you might have of your partner to ensure a seamless production.

Manuscript Prep

Should the narrator read the entire book before beginning recording? That's a great question and one that has several answers.

Some narrators like to read a book through more than once before beginning to record to establish their character choices and make a road map to aid the production. Some narrators who read, or at least look-over, the book before they accept the contract. Others will read through once. Still others will skim the manuscript, looking for plot twists and character surprises. Many will read a few chapters, then record those few chapters, hoping to keep the work fresh and not foreshadow what is to come. Some may choose not to read ahead at all, feeling their performance of the book should mimic the experience of a reader traveling the path with the characters for the first time. All of these methods have their pros and cons, but each narrator will have a preferred method of working. All you need to do is head over to one of the narrator forums on Facebook and you can see this discussed at great length.

An author may feel it's important for a narrator to read the entire text first, and if this is the case, discuss this with the narrator before production begins. Assuming a narrator prepares in any specific way can lead to friction between collaborators. The best course of action is to ask first. Both the author's desires and the narrator's performance process should be respected. As authors, be prepared to hand over the reins, just as a playwright does, and make the space for the narrator's performance to be crafted.

Character Voices

Sometimes, making character voice choices may be impacted by the number of characters in a book. For instance, in Space Opera/Science Fiction, Fantasy, and YA (Young Adult), there can be fifty to a hundred characters, or more—Aliens, humans, inanimate objects, animals—all speaking and interacting. Sigh. We love the creative challenge of a book like that; it stretches the acting muscle way out of the comfort zone.

Some narrators use charts to help them develop and keep track of character voices. These charts will usually have columns for character name, sex, age, nationality, tone, character traits, and the audio file name/number and time code when they first appear. Others use a chart system for marking what voice they use—column one—male/female, column two—low, mid, high, column three—speech quality—gravelly, nasal, lisp, short of breath, etc.

As a side note, Noah is, according to many, very good at accent work, but some narrators struggle with it. The rule of thumb is if a narrator can't do a credible job with an accent, best not to audition for jobs that require it. If a small part rolls around in a project where an accent is required, there are several resources out there. YouTube can be helpful in a pinch. Having someone who is good with accents on speed dial is probably better. Picking one or two small accent qualities or even just enunciating in a slightly different way could work if all else fails.

Turducken

Erin ~ *Here is a little story about figuring out how to do an accent or two. In a book that Noah and I were working on, some of the characters could inhabit each other's bodies.*

In one scene, the hero was having a conversation with the heroine, who had recently been inhabited a bunch of times by their eleven-year-old daughter from the past. The hero, having experienced his daughter being in her mother's body, could sense that there was someone else inside his love, but he didn't know who it was, if it was. When their dialogue begins, she is speaking in her regular voice, but then the hero figures out that he is actually speaking to the villain, at which point the villain drops the pretense of trying to sound like the heroine. But he is still inhabiting her body and using her vocal chords. Are you with me so far? Because reading this back, I'm confused and I lived it.

When we recorded it, I voiced the character a little deeper than her regular voice and with a slightly different cadence than she would normally have. But the author REALLY wanted to have me try to approximate how Noah had been voicing the villain, accent and all. I'm not great with accents. I'm really not great with imitation and Noah had performed the villain with a very deep, gravelly Irish accent. I tried to talk her out of it, but she asked me to please, just try. If it didn't work, we could go back to using the original.

So. Yeah.

Noah and I went into the booth and I said, "Would you just read the first line so I can hear how you would do it?" I tried repeating it with the same accent and cadence he used, but with the character voice I had given the heroine. Eureka! We hit record and started. He would say the line, and I would say it right after him. We recorded the whole scene like that, then went back and edited him out so only my lines of dialogue were left. The author was right. It was so much creepier and so much better that way.

I don't suggest that this is the best way to handle accents you aren't good at, although it worked for us in this instance.

Earlier, we spoke about listening to audiobooks to get a sense of the different styles that are out there. Now is the time for the partners to talk specific style for this specific book. Authors may have a very clear idea of how to read a piece, and narrators may be able to give advice on how to best approach spoken material. It may be clear, from reading our examples below, how we feel about the way an audiobook should be approached, but we are not the ultimate arbiters, just people with some strong opinions.

Some audiobook stylings include:

- ▶ Flat reads with no acting.
- ▶ Lilting reads—under-acting and using voice for a specific sound rather than making strong acting choices.
- ▶ More dramatic, but not overly so, reads that bring you into the story, as if you are watching a movie with no picture.
- ▶ The dreaded hammy read. Melodrama. Insincere. Cartoonish. Where the narrator makes it about their performance rather than about the author's words.

Overacting is a trap any narrator can fall into, especially since they spend so much time sitting in a box alone. The best way to avoid overacting, from a meta perspective, is to take acting classes and learn different methods to play the emotions found in the text. For example, when working on the stage, projecting your voice is important so they can hear you in the nosebleed seats, but with audiobook narration, as the saying goes, "less is more."

Another way is to check in with yourself and ask honest questions. Did that sex scene feel organic, or was the "Oh, God," over the top? Just like with any acting, a narrator will know when it feels right, and when it's pushed too far or becomes artificial. Of course, it always helps to remember how people listen to audiobooks—with headphones, in a car or on a computer. Remembering the "closeness" and intimacy factor can help to guide performance away from ham and toward restrained bliss.

 ### *Did I Get Any On Ya?*

Noah ~ *Performing orgasmic sex scenes is an...interesting thing. We talked earlier about listening back to determine if there's the right amount of heat and sizzle or if you charred the scene to bits. But "getting it right" is an intricate process.*

One of the most frequently asked questions of Romance/Erotica narrators is: "Do you get turned on when you're doing a scene?" Well...to be honest, if the writing is hot...HELL YEAH.

But all of that heat still has to be tempered with the actor's sensibilities. Bringing the scene to climax within the scope of the material presented requires an actor to adjust their performance for this particular medium.

It can become, theoretically, a detriment to let oneself be TOO turned on by the material, to the point where one might scream, "OHHHH GODDDD, DECLAN... OH. MY. GOD." When really, some restraint is needed to make the experience enticing for the listener. It's a melding of unbridled passion and calculated delivery. And that is one of the many, delicious challenges of narrating audiobooks.

PRODUCTION
Technical Specifications

Titles that don't meet these specifications may be rejected by the quality assurance team at ACX. While ACX Quality Control may not catch everything, putting out a shoddy product annoys listeners, tarnishes reputations, and kills sales on the project, not to mention how it reflects on the industry as a whole.

 I'm Sorry, Can You Say That in English?

Erin ~ The technical stuff is usually the information that causes many of us to hire professional post-production teams to do it for us. There is no light and breezy way to explain it. We could just tell you to look at the ACX website, but since we are trying to give you as full a picture as possible, with the information you'll need all in one place, we have added it. Plus, for those of you who feel that you want to do your own post-production work, it is vital information to have.

For several years, I have made efforts to understand engineering. I have looked at online tutorials, I have asked questions of professionals, and, of course, I have paid to take classes. Each time I learn a little bit more but my eyes still glaze over, and my brain flips around inside my head when I read comments in producer's forums, or on technical sites. Engineers toss around words like RMS and stacks and Constant Bit Rate, and I want to know what they mean. I'm not a stupid woman, but somehow the complexities of the technical aspects of my business continue to elude me.

As always, I will continue to work at it, striving to figure it out. But in the meantime, I just wanted to let you know that we tried to make this section as understandable and as pain free as possible. We have identified areas that are "must know," areas that are "good to know," and areas that are for those of you who are autodidacts, mechanically minded, or masochistic. Skip this section if you must, but you do so at your own peril.

Engineering Requirements
MUST KNOW

▶ No uploaded file should be more than 120 minutes in length or 170MB in size. If there is a chapter over this length or size, which has been known to happen occasionally, split it in two. Title the split pieces in such a way that it is clear one chapter is a continuation of the other—for example, "chapter 1a" and "chapter 1b."

▶ Each file must have room tone at the beginning of the file, between half of a second and one second, and at the end, between one second and five seconds. Room tone is the sound of the space without the narrator speaking.

▶ Every file must be a 192kbps or higher MP3, Constant Bit Rate (CBR)[1] at 44.1 kHz[2]. You set these in your DAW when you go to render or export your file.

GOOD TO KNOW

▶ Constant Bit Rate is an encoding standard for audio files that forces all of a codec's output data to be uniform. This is easily accomplished by verifying the settings are correct when converting the wav files from your raw record to mp3's for upload.

AUTODIDACT AND MASOCHIST

▶ A codec is a device or program that compresses data to enable faster transmission and decompresses received data.

---

1 http://www.acx.com/help/acx-audio-submission-requirements/201456300#192kbps-MP3
2 http://www.acx.com/help/acx-audio-submission-requirements/201456300#44.1-kHz

Enhanced Experience

Some of the requirements are there to enhance listener experience.

MUST KNOW

▶ All uploaded files need to be consistent in overall sound and formatting.

▶ All uploaded chapters must be all mono or all stereo files. Imagine how the overall production might be impacted if this is inconsistent.

▶ Uploaded files must contain only one chapter or section.

▶ Files must have the section header read aloud as they are part of the manuscript, this allows the listener to know where they are in the book.

▶ Finished files must be "free of noise," other than the noise of the performance.

GOOD TO KNOW

▶ "Noise-free" performances include both sounds the narrator might make, like mouth clicks, plosives (hard P or C-type sounds that make a boom-ish noise on the recording), fabric swishing, stomach gurgles, and sounds that come from the environment that might not be heard as the recording in being done—computer fans, air conditioner, unknown thuds, or the refrigerator motor.

▶ The project must be narrated by an actual human being. So, those of you who are worried about improved artificial intelligence and enhanced text to speech programs, you can take a deep breath and go about your business.

Industry Standards
MUST KNOW

▶ Every project must include opening and closing credits, which are supplied by ACX. The author may add to them or adjust them.

▶ Finished projects must include a retail sample between one and five minutes long.

▶ Every file must measure between -23dB and -18dB RMS[1].

GOOD TO KNOW

▶ The retail sample is used as a preview to market the book on platforms like Audible and Amazon. These should not include chapter headings or credits and must not contain any explicit material even if the narrator is narrating a genre that specifically contains graphic depictions of sex or violence. Authors, think carefully about what is most likely to lure customers to want to buy your book, and you'll know what your retail sample should be.

AUTODIDACT AND MASOCHIST

▶ Root Mean Square (RMS) is the average loudness of the entire file. It is measured by meters that are part of the Digital Audio Workstation and have -3dB peak values. Peak Values are how loud the file is at its loudest. A maximum -60dB noise floor, the level of the noise that exists below the audio signal in decibels (dB), is measured by recording the room tone and looking for the audible level of noise with no narration.

You Don't Have to Be a Rocket Scientist.

Noah ~ *I've worked on about fifty ACX projects. In the early days, I was doing the editing and mastering myself. While I may be tech savvy in certain ways, as I think I mentioned earlier, recording software intricacies elude me. When I see the terms like "RMS" and "dB," I'm thinking it has something to do with dungeon porn. So, I learned to do just enough to make my projects sound good and be acceptable under ACX standards.*

---

1 http://www.acx.com/help/acx-audio-submission-requirements/201456300#RMS

I listen to each chapter, the sound of my own voice lulling me into a mindless stupor, and "cut" errant sounds, shorten or lengthen silences between sentences for flow and dramatic effect, apply a patch of room tone here and there, and then "master" my files with two simple effects: Leveling at -70db (whatever the heck that is) and Normalizing at -3 or -5 dB, depending on how loud I was during the recording. These tools I learned from talking with my friend Gary.

Remember him?

There was so much more I could have done but didn't really understand how to do. You know what? All of those audiobooks are just fine. When I listen to them, it's hard to tell the difference between the overall quality of my rag-tag produced projects and Audible's professionally edited and mastered ones.

I'm not saying there isn't a difference. There certainly is, but to most untrained ears and on most listening devices, the difference may not be noticeable.

What's my point? Oh, yeah, my point is that you don't have to be a master engineer to put out good-quality audiobooks. Your projects will be better with more knowledge of editing and mastering techniques, even if only for a specific set of ears that can tell the difference. So, be proficient with the basics, and if you have the time and desire, learn the more intricate aspects, or if you can afford it, FIO (Farm It Out) to an audiobook editing professional.

Performance Techniques

One listener's favorite narrating style is another person's unbearable, outrageously bad, unlistenable dreck. Those who work alone may not realize they're carried away by the words, and think they're "helping" the listener by over-emphasizing certain ones in a consciously onomatopoeic way or by actually screaming when the author has written, "he screamed." Remember, as the narrator, you're speaking directly into someone's ear. Your performance should be truthful and thoughtful. How do these characters feel instead of how do the words sound? The narrator's volume needs to be consistent and appropriate for the medium.

Understanding a little bit about working with a mic can be helpful in that regard. Sometimes the narrator will come across a character who whispers. If the mic is too far from the mouth, those sensual growls may sound like wind blowing in the trees. If the mic is too close to the mouth, that provocative purring may sound more like an evil phantasm. Shouting into a mic can cause distortion, otherwise known as clipping, which can ruin a recording. A narrator who stands too far from the mic could sound like Uncle Murray in the bathroom calling for a roll of toilet paper. It is possible to have the energy of yelling without the volume of yelling. It's possible to use a combination of mic distance and voice modulation, so the result is audible but has the same feeling and intent of an actual whisper. Yup. Acting skills. Again.

A combination of mic technique and voice control goes a long way to convey the various emotions in a story, be it in a whisper or a scream, and may be the difference between someone loving the audiobook, and someone not being able to listen to it.

Sound Effects and Music
A quick word about music, sound effects, and other special features. For authors and actors who want to enhance their audiobook with aural accouterment, there are a few things to keep in mind and to discuss before production begins:

▶ Are you legally able to use the piece of music or sound effect?

▶ Are you judicious about the use of sound effects to enhance the listener's experience and not distract them?

▶ Will the music/efx be properly leveled and blended with the narration?

Also, remember that different listeners react differently to music and sound effects. If the author or narrator plans on using any of these devices, have some friends or audiobook enthusiasts preview a chapter or two and see what they think.

THE FIRST FIFTEEN (TFF)

ONCE ALL THE PRE-PRODUCTION COMMUNICATION HAS taken place, and both partners are on the same page, ACX requires the narrator to submit an audio sample to the author before full production can commence. This sample is referred to as "The First Fifteen Minutes."

Prior to recording The First Fifteen, the author will hopefully have supplied the narrator with a character bible and pronunciation guide.

This communication gives both the author and the narrator a solid place from which to spring forward smoothly and successfully. During this pre-production period, it is possible to iron out all the major character voices through phone conversations, written communication, and short recordings made by the narrator for the author. Then, the narrator can record TFF of the book, submit it to the author, and the production can begin.

If the major voices are not agreed on ahead of time, and the actual First Fifteen Minutes of the manuscript does not contain the most important characters, TFF can be a great opportunity to work out these details.

Otherwise, the author may receive a completed project with voices and pacing that sound all wrong to them.

We stress this because once The First Fifteen Minutes are approved, the narrator has the agreement of the author to complete the project. That's exciting and wonderful, but there is the potential for misunderstanding and miscommunication in the partner relationship.

To avoid misalignment, authors can select passages from the book that are particularly important in terms of tone, character, and pace, and use those in place of the actual first fifteen minutes of the manuscript. These passages do not have to be contiguous, they can come from a variety of chapters, but should add up to around fifteen minutes of finished audio. Depending on typeface and spacing, this could be around 2000 to 2500 words.

Once The First Fifteen has been submitted, the author can simply "accept" the submission, or "reject" it and let the narrator know what they feel needs to be addressed, though if the partners have been communicating well throughout, this won't happen often. Contractually, the author has the right to ask the narrator to re-do TFF up to two times, if necessary.

Lastly, if author and narrator are going to work in collaboration, TFF will give both partners a good sense of whether they will work well together or not. If things are not going well, this is the point at which both parties should cut their losses and walk away. ACX will not punish either if this happens before The First Fifteen Minutes are approved. It could, however, be costly for the author to dissolve the contract at a later date, once most or all of the recording is completed. According to the ACX contract, there will be termination fees due to the narrator in this case. These are discussed in the later section titled "When Things Go Wrong."

PRODUCTION

A couple of important points pertaining to The First Fifteen.

Authors' Rights of Approval
ACX sets out that authors have three rights of approval:

1. Choosing a narrator/producer.
2. The First Fifteen.
3. The Final Production.

Other than these three instances, the narrator has a mostly free rein to produce the audiobook as they feel it will best suit the material.

Within the narrator community, there are different styles of producing. The two main camps are Autonomous and Collaborators. Both are good and valid styles.

Autonomous Production Style
Some of the best and most experienced narrators in the business prefer to do what they do with very little outside input. These are audiobook professionals who put out awesome experiences for the listeners. There are many authors who prefer this style. They may not have time to be involved with the ongoing production and just want to get the finished product when it's...you know, finished.

Collaborative Production Style
The three of us love the collaborative creative process. There are lots of authors and narrators out there who do as well. We like to roll ideas off each other, share in the funny and difficult moments, and we believe that a great end result comes from the meeting of minds.

So, for those in the more autonomous group, TFF is especially import-ant. With these narrator/producers, once TFF is approved, the author probably won't hear from them again until project completion. Getting those important voices and pacing agreed upon at this point is critical. For those who prefer the school of collaboration, issues can be worked out as they come up during the production process. So this is another one of the many decisions authors and narrators need to make going into this business. Which style is right for you?

Who's Running This Show?

Noah ~ *Narrators all have their own thoughts on how much involvement an author could or should have in an audiobook project. For me, audiobook production is in some ways much like any other branch of the entertainment industry. I don't have a ton of film and TV acting credits. I have fewer film and TV Producing credits, but I've worked in and been around the entertainment business for most of my life.*

The term "producer" can mean many different things, from one who actually takes part in and makes a production happen to some schmo who said, "Don't call it Terminator...call it THE Terminator" and got a producer credit for his trouble.

However, the term, "Executive Producer," at least to my mind, has a much narrower meaning. This individual either puts up or is responsible for someone else fronting "The Money." This position, from my experience, comes with a certain amount of sway over how that money is spent.

What does this have to do with audiobooks? Unlike publishing houses that produce audiobooks and have ample funds, the independent author is, perhaps, scrounging through their pockets, among the candy wrappers, old receipts, and slack lint, to come up with the money to pay for a PFH production audiobook

They are the executive producer.

So, for me, this holds some weight and influences how I run my business. It makes it that much more important to me to offer the opportunity for an author to collaborate, in some way, on the production for which they are paying. That it is often fun and fulfilling is a side-benefit.

I don't feel that those who are more on the autonomous side are wrong. Heaven knows many of them are more successful than am I. I just prefer my way of doing business.

Manuscript Flaws

As an author, hearing your words performed aloud for the first time can be an anxious experience. You'll hear every flaw in your writing. Every repeated word, every missed weak verb. Every poorly structured sentence. It will get easier every time you listen, but this can be a soul-crushing experience for a writer. Use this knowledge to improve your craft in the future, but understand, the audio production is not a time to edit the manuscript. Don't ask your narrator to fix the flaws in your writing. They are narrators, not editors. Some may be willing to edit for an additional fee, while others may flat out refuse, and rightfully so, since this makes the entire process slower and more expensive for them.

Exquisite

Renea ~ *When I listen to Noah and Erin perform my books now, it's an enjoyable experience. I look forward to reviewing the production, and this is how I envisioned it would always be. But it wasn't always so.*

I had what I could only label a bit of a crisis of faith when first listening to Curing Doctor Vincent. Noah and Erin were wonderful, engaging, and added dimension to the story that went well beyond my words. What I didn't prepare myself for was that, while text is very forgiving, audio is not.

With text, you can get away with a sloppy word here or there, a redundant phrase or awkward sentence, and it usually won't trip up the reader. In audio, let's say that one of your characters has a word he likes to say often. Let's use the word "exquisite" for example. Someone reading the text may never notice that Xavier says it fifty-two times in a 51,000-word book. OK, that's a bit of an exaggeration, but he says it a lot. In text, it's simply another descriptor, but when you hear Noah in his smooth and sexy Dr. V voice tell Elaine she's exquisite, it really stands out, and when he does it again, and again, and again... Sigh. This one word became quite the inside joke with us. That and nipple twisting.

During that first production, I heard every redundant word, every repeated phrase, every awkward sentence, and Noah and Erin are so good, they even made some of my sins sound forgivable. But I wondered if I had made the right call. Should I have ever been a writer at all? Was I too weak to write books for audio? I can confidently say I'm doing exactly what I should be, now that I have some distance and experience, but geesh...the experience was rough.

Now, I just listen for those errors, drink some wine, and use the knowledge to improve my craft. But that first book was a tough one.

Reasonable Edits

Sometimes a narrator's eyes see words that aren't on the page. As they read along, acting the parts and being immersed in the work, they may, inadvertently, add or change a word. Some authors are OK with this, as long as it doesn't change the meaning of the sentence. However, an author contracts with a narrator to read exactly what is written on the page. It is perfectly acceptable for an author to require an exact match of their book, but they need to remember this will include any misprints, editing mistakes/oversights that appear in the manuscript. As with any business relationship, a reasonable approach is important. Empathy, our friends, is a good thing.

Really? Again? I Told You, It's Pronounced "Sha-DAY"!

Erin ~ Sometimes reasonable edits are really annoying, for instance, those darn pronunciation mistakes. What was an easily avoidable error can become lots of additional work for a narrator.

I recently had the great pleasure to work on a series with multiple narrators. Each one of us narrated the chapters from our character's point of view.

The book contains an ancillary character named Xavier. I grew up with a friend whose father's name was Xavier, pronounced Zae-vee-er, so that was how I pronounced the character's name. One of the other narrators had a friend named Xavier, pronounced Ex-ay-vee-er, so that was how he pronounced the character's name.

When I got my notes back from quality control at the production company, I had fifty-two issues that needed to be re-recorded. Fifty-two! I was beside myself. Some of them were the typical added or dropped word. It turned out that the majority of the fifty-two were changing Zae-vee-er to Ex-ay-vee-er, because the other narrator said the name more frequently than I did in the text.

FROM RECORDING TO COMPLETION

NOW, FOR YOUR READING OR LISTENING PLEASURE—AN interlude. Just kidding. A timeline of how the process works in real time, or at least, how we do it.

▶ Narrators record.

▶ Files get edited and mastered (Editor and/or engineer provides pickups with timestamp and page numbers in the PDF).

▶ Finished files are uploaded to ACX for author review and additional QC.

▶ Author returns notes, if any, with audio timestamp(s), PDF page(s) and correction or suggestion to be made.

▶ Process continues until all material is recorded, fixed, and re-uploaded.

▶ Narrator clicks, "I'M DONE" on ACX.

▶ Author approves (if appropriate) and sends ACX-calculated payment to narrator via their pre-agreed-upon method.

▶ Once funds are received, narrator acknowledges so on ACX.

▶ The production is officially finished, and the audiobook goes into the ACX system for processing on its way to retail.

That's the nuts and bolts of it. It's pretty straightforward. Again, how smoothly this process goes depends on great communication, lots of "getting agreement" on things ahead of time, establishing a smooth workflow, and addressing issues as soon as they come up, rather than waiting until later.

FROM COMPLETION TO RETAIL

THE RECORDING IS DONE. QC, EDITING, AND MASTERing... Done! The author has approved and paid, and the narrator has received payment and acknowledged such on ACX. Or both parties have agreed to share the royalties. You both get the happy message that says your audiobook is "Headed to retail!" Now what?

The good people at ACX will tell you the time to retail is ten to fourteen business days, and they do their best to keep their word. Depending on the time of year, it could take longer before the audiobook appears on Amazon, Audible, and iTunes.

During the fall, for example, in the run-up to the holiday season or in the late spring, in preparation for summer travel sales, the ACX production system can become backed up, and an audiobook could take longer to release in the retail channel. The shortest amount of time we've seen is five days and the longest, a little over four weeks. Rest assured; ACX will get the audiobook through their system as quickly as they possibly can.

While you're waiting, instead of listening to "on-hold music," how about doing some marketing? You didn't think that just because the audiobook was done that you were done, did you?

MARKETING

WORK SHOULDN'T BE THIS MUCH FUN

THOUGHTFUL PROMOTIONS

BEING REVIEWED

THESE ARE A FEW OF MY FAVORITE ZINGS

REVIEWER IN TROLL CLOTHING

TAKE IT WITH A GRAIN OF SALT THE SIZE OF CLEVELAND

REVIEWERS

BUNDLING BOOKS

MARKETING RESOURCES

NOW THAT WEEKS TO MONTHS OF COLLABORATION HAVE come to an end, it's time to let the world listen to your efforts.

If you're an author on a sales-driven journey, promotion is part of the path, but whether or not your narrator takes part in that journey depends on many factors.

Unless the narrator expressly agreed to co-market the book, as should ostensibly be done with RS deals, there may not be any incentive for them to continue on the journey with you. In a PFH contract, there is no direct financial benefit to helping you sell your book. There are many indirect benefits, such as networking, publicity, and repeat business, but whether these are incentives depends on the narrator's personal style and goals.

Some narrators embrace publicity, while others would rather close the project and move on. Still, many may be open to situational promotion. The best way to gauge the narrator's desire to promote is to have an open and frank conversation. If you'd like your narrator to be part of your marketing plan and round out your audiobook team, by all means, invite them to do so, but unless they have expressly agreed to help market, do not rely on them to be part of your success plan.

From our experience, narrators working PFH rates reap the benefits of new, sometimes rabid fans and followers from taking part in promotions. As a narrator actively growing your business and trying to build out your portfolio and popularity with your audience, having a proven track record of wanting to help authors succeed is attractive to other authors looking to do audiobooks. Growing a fan base and enthusiasm for a partner's success may not, necessarily, help a narrator when it comes to booking contract work with traditional audiobook publishing companies, but it sure won't hurt, either. These companies do appreciate narrators who maintain great relationships with authors. This engagement helps the author you're promoting sell more books, which could lead to more audiobooks. The symbiosis and inter-dependent relationship is powerful!

Work Shouldn't Be This Much Fun

Noah ~ *Erin and I had SUCH a great time working on Renea's books. The stories are wonderful, the characters compelling and...well...they're hot. During recording, we cracked up so much with the mistakes we made that we came out with two "outtakes" reels. So when Renea, marketing wiz that she is, asked us to take part in some promotional activities, we were like, "Um...hell YEAH!"*

I think the first one was an FB, online "Release Party" for the audiobook of Curing Doctor Vincent. Renea's fans, The Mad Masons, are incredible. Very devoted to her work. So, Renea set up the event. The three of us talked about how it would be structured and then, on "The Night of," Renea was wherever she is when she does these things, a glass of good red in hand, no doubt, and Erin and I were at my place, each on a different computer, each with our libation of choice at the ready.

When things kicked off, Renea introduced us. Then...the questions started. We were being peppered so fast with things Renea's fans wanted to know, I think both Erin and I got "thumb lock" from typing so rapidly. I eventually ditched the computer I was using and answered from my phone, instead.

"What's it like recording sex scenes?"

"Do you get embarrassed?"

"Do you get turned on?"

"What's the hardest part about narrating?"

"Who was the nineteenth President?"

OK, nobody asked that last question. But the group was so warm and welcoming and interested and fun and enthusiastic. It was a blast. One of the "activities" in the event was to have an audience-written scene. Renea set the stage—characters, setting, etc., and then the group took turns writing lines of dialogue, action, etc. After the event was over, Erin and I took all that stuff and recorded it as a short story for the fans. It was so much fun. We've done a couple of those events, plus a recorded interview using questions submitted by Renea's fans. And Renea posted both of our outtakes reels on her website.

It's great to get paid for doing what you love—but to take part in events like these, to help an author promote the audiobooks, and make new friends and fans, it's really amazing.

THOUGHTFUL PROMOTIONS
WHEN CO-PROMOTING, BOTH PARTIES SHOULD ALWAYS BE mindful of the tone and methods used when reaching the audience. Authors work very hard to build and maintain their reader bases. They spend not just time but also considerable money putting on events, attending conferences, and interacting with potential and existing readers. It is of utmost importance the relationship between author and reader/listener be respected, as should the relationship between narrator and listener. It's obviously counterproductive and potentially damaging for either side to promote in a way that may adversely affect the other.

Discuss the different platforms each partner plans to use and the strategy for each of those platforms. One of you may be a wiz at setting up Facebook events, while the other may be really great at doing Instagram videos. Agree on what kind of information will go out over which platform, who will write what kind of posts, and what the timing of posts should be.

Facebook is kind of like a backyard barbecue. You have the leisure to make contact, have conversations, and share a little bit about yourself. Twitter is a great place to share pertinent information and newsworthy items. LinkedIn should be used for professional purposes only—don't post personal information. Instagram is a great way to peek into someone's world. Making short videos that show who you are and how your process works can help to educate your audiences. Snapchat is silly and fun and can be used to keep in touch with super fans and make them feel special. Please note, no one, not even the biggest fans, wants to see the same generic promotional posts seven times a day. They like variety, substance, and engagement. Give them something interesting to connect with them.

BEING REVIEWED

IT'S TRUE THAT WE'RE MORE APT TO BELIEVE WHAT WE ARE told by people who are like us than we are to believe the promotional material that comes from authors or narrators. Getting reviews, hopefully positive ones, is one way to increase buzz about the title. In the best of all worlds, you make the audiobook, it goes on sale, and millions of adoring fans listen, love it, and write glowing reviews. That's a lovely idea. The reality is that if the book doesn't have a large fan following in ebook format, it may take more than just having it go on sale to get people to spread the good news about the release.

Unless you're a first-time author or brand new narrator, you're probably familiar with reviews. They can either make your day or have you pouring wine to the brim. We three don't mind bad reviews, as long as there's passion in the reviewer's opinion or solid, constructive criticism. As artists, we love to evoke emotions. After all, that is what acting and writing is all about, right? And hatred is a perfectly valid emotion.

A bad audiobook review for an author is no fun, but in a sense, the author is a step removed from the outcome. The author is not "released" from responsibility for the outcome, but after their book has been written, edited, and beta-read, it's been through a pretty strong vetting process, where various people have already voiced their opinions of the work. Considering the success or failure of an audiobook can depend on the narration, the author is not necessarily as directly or personally attached as the narrator may be.

As a narrator, your voice is an extension of you. A bad audiobook review can feel at times like someone making a derogatory comment about your hair or weight, or some other physical attribute. That can sting and require some thick skin to remain focused on your career goals.

 These Are a Few Of My Favorite Zings
Erin ~ *Here are a few of my other "favorite" reviews:*

"The narrator was horrible. She sounded like she was doing a baby voice the whole time...which made the sex scenes beyond uncomfortable—downright pedophilic."

"I can't focus on the content because I feel like the narrator is trying to sound seductive. Seriously, she is definitely not suited to inspire females by reading a book about loving yourself using seductive energy in reading."

"I really like the way this book is narrated, I just do not like the female, Erin. One of these days, I will remember not to buy the books she narrates. She talks so low it gets on my nerves. This book would be one of the ones that I like to listen to if not for Erin. Will have to return."

Because readers may have preconceived notions about what characters should sound like, especially those who read the print or ebook before listening to the audio, reviewers tend to be more critical of narrators. This extra scrutiny can be especially true of female narrators in the Romance genres. Listeners of Romance/Erotica tend to be female. Perhaps if the voice they hear in their ears is one that is hard for them to relate to personally, they are less forgiving. So, for the ladies in "The Booth," don't take these comments too much to heart.

 ### Reviewer in Troll Clothing

Renea ~ Everyone remembers their first bad review. Luckily for me, I cut my writing teeth on a website where strangers reviewed and critiqued my work for points. Not only did that experience lead to some lifelong friendships, but it also prepared me for the phenomenon that happens when someone can sit anonymously behind a keyboard and unleash their opinions without repercussions. Yes, letting strangers on the Internet read your unpolished work is about as pleasant as you'd expect—somewhere up there with a root canal. Regardless, the experience was invaluable, and I'd recommend the process to anyone.

When that first vitriol-filled review popped up, I searched for the teachable portions of it. Fortunately, the first couple contained such moments. It felt very much like the crass and harsh critiques I'd received in the early days, so it didn't bother me. I learned and then moved on.

Then came the day when I got the first personal attack. The review had nothing to do with my book but attacked my character based on a piece of fiction I wrote. I, admittedly, was unsettled. Then came something even worse—the dreaded one-star with no explanation. These reviews affect your overall rating, but provide no feedback so I can learn. I'd rather hear the personal attack, than nothing at all.

One day, sometime later, I stumbled upon a thread in a Facebook group. It was not filled with your typical tenacious readers who frequent author groups and engage with authors online. These were your average readers who read maybe a book a month at most.

Several important pieces of information came to light. The first was that many of them don't write reviews at all, and of those that did, they had no idea the author of the book may actually read their review. Many of them saw it as a way to vent their frustration with the story, but never actually considered the person who wrote it might read it and be hurt by it.

Something else interesting involved sites like Goodreads, where there are no real controls around reviews. Several people in the group said that they didn't realize the star ratings reflected poorly on an author's rating, and they used those star ratings not necessarily as a rating for the book, but as a way to organize their book lists.

This discussion gave me some better insight into the behavior of reviewers, especially those who don't do it often. I tend to be someone who likes to assume positive intentions, so now those one-stars may not be evil Internet trolls after all. Even though it's never a good thing to attack someone's character without knowing them, especially based on a piece of fiction they wrote, it's a little easier to tolerate when you see it as venting.

With all that said, some of my best reviews are my worst ones, since they challenge me to be a better writer.

Some audiobook reviewers may be singularly focused in their review summary, heaping their praise or condemnation on only the author or the narrator. This single-sidedness can make the other partner feel left out, especially when the star ratings reflect the singular focus. For example, if the listener hated the narration, they may give one or two stars across the board, not rating the story separately.

Learning to distance yourself will become very important. Reviews are not necessarily a reflection of your talents as authors and narrators. Constructive bad reviews can be exceptionally helpful, but even with those, unless you hear the same comment several times, be hesitant to make changes to your style based on a sole piece of feedback. However, carefully consider the criticism you hear several times as an improvement opportunity. So be open to what they are saying. It could help you on your next project. We all have those areas we're working on, and practice does make better, as the saying goes, but ignore anyone who attacks your work based their opinion or personal experiences and preferences. Taste is individual and subjective, and though people can sometimes be cruel with words, don't allow them to affect you too deeply. Always keep a few grains of salt handy, and remember narration preference is much like music preference. Some people are just not going to like country music, no matter how talented the musicians. The same goes for writers, narrators, and genres.

If all else fails, look up a book narrated by someone famous you admire. You'll see the same mix of reviews for them. We're all in this together. Bad reviews are, unfortunately, universal.

Take It with A Grain of Salt the Size of Cleveland

Noah ~ Here's an amusing anecdote illustrating why not-so-good reviews should be taken with a grain of salt. A BIG one. A reviewer railed about how bad a narrator was. We'll call them

Narrator "A." The reviewer of this non-Romance audiobook felt A was so bad that they weren't able to finish listening. They went on to say the audiobook would have been infinitely better if the narrator was their favorite Romance narrator. We'll call this narrator, Narrator "B."

Unbeknownst to this reviewer and much to their embarrassment, if they ever found out...you know what's coming next, don't you? Yup, narrator A and B were the same person, just using different names for different genres. It's a funny world, isn't it?

REVIEWERS

THERE ARE SEVERAL WAYS TO FIND PEOPLE TO REVIEW YOUR audiobook. Some of them cost money and take less time and effort on your part, and some cost nothing, yet require a lot of energy and creativity.

There are services you can purchase to help you reach reviewers. Some will give you ways to use your ACX codes, so you're more likely to get your book reviewed using these services than you are by offering codes as part of a giveaway or to people who may use your code for another author's audiobook. There is usually a modest fee for these types of services. Others provide virtual tours of book blogs and guarantee a certain number of reviews for the price of the tour. Not all tour services are the same, so be sure to ask around before booking one, as they can be pricey. Plus, they don't even give you lunch on the trip!

Another way of trying to get your audiobook reviewed is to search the Internet for bloggers who review in your genre. Some bloggers will take unsolicited audiobooks and provide honest reviews. Some bloggers will only review materials they have personally asked for and will only accept certain genres. Make sure you keep track of which is which. Those who don't take unsolicited materials will not be pleased to receive your audiobook, even if it's free. You will want to build a relationship with these bloggers and let them approach you about your work.

The best way to get reviews is to build long-term relationships with listeners and the way you find those involves a solid marketing plan.

BUNDLING BOOKS

WHAT IS A BUNDLE AND WHY WOULD I WANT TO DO IT? Let's say you have written ten novellas and they all have a similar theme or share characters. You might choose to create one new book out of the ten short ones. Why? Because people who buy audiobooks tend to prefer to spend their money or credits on full-length books, it's a much better use of resources—more bang for the buck.

So, how does one create a bundle? ACX and Audible are pretty strict when it comes to repurposing material that has already been recorded. There are several posts on the ACX site that detail how to do this, but here is what we have learned:

The first thing to know is that before you can bundle your audio, you must bundle your print or ebook versions and they must be listed on Amazon.com. This new bundled version will be a new product that you can use to post on ACX to start the project.

Authors who decide to bundle stories negotiate a separate price with their narrators just for the project. Because the narrator will take existing audio files, give them new chapter headings, record new opening and closing credits, and then upload the whole project, it will take far less time than the original recording and post work did. This price can be a flat fee or an hourly rate for actual hours of studio time put into the project. Each partnership will need to carefully discuss what is affordable and fair, conditions which will be different for each set of partners and each project proposed.

Be mindful that authors are only supposed to have one bundle per series. So if you are an author who thinks they might want to bundle, wait until all your pieces are in place before posting. Once you've bundled a series, ACX will not let you re-bundle in a different formation. The bundle must contain all the books and be uploaded as one project.

If the audiobooks you wish to bundle were paid for through an RS contract, you must use the same narrator for each of the books throughout the bundle. The reason behind this rule is purely financial. When an author enters into an RS contract with a narrator, they agree to split the royalties earned on the recordings for seven years. It doesn't matter if the recording is a standalone novella or is part of a bundle. If there were multiple narrators in a bundle, it would be very difficult and time consuming to figure out how to split the royalties. If you paid for your audiobooks using a PFH contract, you can have books within the bundle with different narrators. Audiobook listeners tend to like the same narrator throughout a series, so this might not be the best way to go, but if you've already recorded the books with different narrators, it will be what it will be.

MARKETING RESOURCES

FROM SOCIAL MEDIA TO WEBSITES TO READER ENGAGEment, when you start the audiobook journey, there will be many different ways you will need to market your audiobook.

Because the audiobook industry is growing so rapidly, marketing concepts that worked yesterday may not work today or tomorrow. Staying nimble, always learning and assessing, will be key to your success.

The "Promote Yourself" section of the ACX.com website[1] and the ACX Blog are valuable sources of information that advise authors and narrators to have a strong audiobook web presence. Resources include audiobook pages, samples, things like outtakes, YouTube and Soundcloud clips, and more.

Below is a list of ideas and resources we've come across while flexing our promotion muscles.

Co-promotion

Promote with your fellow authors and narrators. You can co-host events, plan giveaways and coordinate blog posts. When an individual loves a genre, even if they have a favorite author, they will seek out other books and audiobooks in that genre. Teaming up can help both parties. There are also opportunities for authors to co-promote with other authors who use the same narrators to help encourage readership crossover.

ACX.com

Don't forget to start with your ACX profile, if you're a narrator. Check out Noah and Erin's here.

- Noah – https://www.acx.com/narrator?p=A7143UD7LOGB0
- Erin – https://www.acx.com/narrator?p=AH3BT52XGHXP3

Websites

Be sure to have a page that showcases your audiobooks. You can check out our websites to see how we feature our audiobook work.

- Renea's Website – http://ReneaMason.com

---

1 https://www.acx.com/help/promote-yourself/200485310

▶ Noah's Website – http://NoahMichaelLevine.com

▶ Erin's Website – http://www.erindeward.com/

Newsletters

As an author or narrator builds an audience, newsletters give you the most control over getting your important communications to your reader/listenership. The power of the newsletter is that it isn't subject to rules like Facebook. You have 10,000 "likes" on Facebook, but Facebook gets to decide who sees your message. It's important to have people who *want* to be part of your newsletter on your list and to engage with your newsletter subscribers by offering exclusive content, giveaways, and other promotions. MailChimp and Mad Mimi are two popular newsletter management programs, and they are both easy to use.

Facebook

FACEBOOK ADS

Facebook ads are a great way to gain momentum, but they can also be an easy way to sink money fast into something that doesn't gain you much. Research and understand your genre. Use the targeting features in the Ad Manager to hone in on readers who like authors with books most similar to the work you have produced and want to produce in the future.

FACEBOOK PARTIES AND EVENTS

Participate in Facebook parties associated with audiobooks, especially launches. As a team, we've participated in more than a few events together. You can check out the link here:

http://reneamason.com/media-appearences/

FACEBOOK PAGES

There are many audiobook related Facebook pages that you may be able to collaborate with. Plus, don't forget to set up your own. Here are our own and a few other examples, but there are many more.

- Renea's Page – https://www.facebook.com/ReneaMasonAuthor/
- Noah's Page – https://www.facebook.com/TheNoahMichaelLevine/
- Erin's Page – https://www.facebook.com/erindewardaudiobooks/

Other audiobook focused Facebook Pages

- ACX.com – https://www.facebook.com/goacx/
- Aural Fixation – https://www.facebook.com/auralfixationaudio/
- Audio Hottie – https://www.facebook.com/audiohottie

FACEBOOK ACCOUNT/PROFILE
Sometimes Facebook makes it difficult to reach your followers using pages, but you can also use your personal account/profile to attract listeners. You can set your security high for posts for your "true" friends, while making public posts as well, to allow your account to accumulate followers. You will need to turn on the "allow followers" feature in Facebook settings. When someone sends you a friend request, and you'd rather not have them use up one of your limited 5000 friend slots, delete the friend request instead of confirming, and the requester will be automatically added to your list of followers. Deleting is a good thing to do with when you receive friend requests from people who might have suspicious looking profiles. Using your profile can expand your reach beyond your Facebook page.

If you use a pseudonym, be careful using multiple Facebook accounts, since Facebook may require you to prove your identity. So even though it may seem like a good idea to set up multiple accounts, every so often Facebook becomes finicky about this rule and many authors have permanently lost access to their accounts and therefore their audience.

▶ Renea's Profile – https://www.facebook.com/S.ReneaMason
▶ Noah's Profile – https://www.facebook.com/noah.m.levine.3

FACEBOOK GROUPS
Join one of the following Facebook groups for audiobook lovers. You can find even more by typing the name of the group into the Facebook search box.

Join or create a networking group to help build a better audiobook community, such as:

▶ The Audiobook Book Community Support Group
https://www.facebook.com/groups/
TheAudioBookBookCommunitySupportGroup/

Other audiobook focused groups:

▶ Aural Fixation –
https://www.facebook.com/groups/auralfixationaudio/
▶ Audible Addicts –
https://www.facebook.com/groups/audiobookaddicts/
▶ Audiobooks Romance and Erotica –
https://www.facebook.com/groups/audiobookseroticromance/

Create a fan group where you can interact with your listeners. The members of Renea's Mad Mason Friends and Readers Group support her in so many ways. Must be 18 years or older to join.

▶ https://www.facebook.com/groups/TheMadMasons/

Instagram

Noah sometimes does short Instagram videos to give a behind the scenes look to listeners and to make special book announcements. You can visit our profiles by searching for:

- ▶ @therealbadnoah
- ▶ @renea_mason
- ▶ @erindeward

Other audiobook related Instagram accounts:

- ▶ @auralfixationfb
- ▶ @theaudioflow

Twitter

Twitter is a great place to post fast and catchy headlines. Twitter is also an ideal method of grabbing someone's attention. Build networking relationships by commenting on and sharing posts closely related to yours. You can also create or attend Twitter parties using unique hashtags.

- ▶ Follow us on Twitter - @ReneaMason1 @badnoah @Erindeward
- ▶ Other audiobook related Twitter accounts to check out - @acx_com @auralfixationfb @audio_hottie

Hashtag Promos

Hashtagging your promotions during key months can help you gain visibility, especially in June, audiobook month. #fall4audio, #springflingaudio, #snowaudio, and #xmasaudio are all hashtags that have been used for past promotions.

Crowdspeaking Platforms

You have probably seen support on social media asking others to support their Thunderclap or Headtalker. These programs allow authors and narrators to pool the social media resources of everyone who supports the campaign. So, instead of posting your new release promotion to your Facebook page and profile, it will be posted to all of the social media pages, profiles, and platforms of those that supported your campaign, and at the same time giving you a greater audience reach. However, many of these programs require a minimum number of supporters to actually work. Thunderclap, for example, requires a hundred supporters.

Spotlights, Interviews, and Podcasts
Participating in spotlights, interviews, podcasts, and review sites puts you in front of audiences who have no previous exposure to your work. Podcasts, especially because of their audio delivery, are great for audiobook promotions. You can always search the Internet for new opportunities, since new ones pop up all the time.

- Podcast – https://www.spreaker.com/show/the-audio-flow

YouTube
Put your audio clips on YouTube. Limit them to fifteen minutes or less. YouTube is also a great place for book trailers and video blogs. Pay attention to what keywords you use during uploads, and use terms that make it easy for people to find your video.

- Noah – http://www.youtube.com/eleuthra
- Renea – http://www.youtube.com/c/ReneaMason

SoundCloud
Put your audio clips on SoundCloud. This platform is a useful place to share narrator audition clips.

- Noah – http://www.soundcloud.com/eleuthra

- ▸ Erin – https://soundcloud.com/erin-deward
- ▸ Renea – https://soundcloud.com/reneamason

Audible Clips
Audible has a way to share snippets of audiobooks. Post these clips on social media and encourage your readers to do so, too.

30-Day Audible Free Trial
Don't forget that Audible offers a 30-day free trial membership. This offering can come in handy when promoting. If your book is the first one downloaded and the listener keeps the service for ninety days, not only do you get the book sale, but the $50 Bounty, or $25 if you are in an RS contract.

Groupon/LivingSocial and Other Discount Promo Code Sites
Audible often does special promotions through discount sites. You can, in some cases, gift these discounted subscriptions to your listeners for promotion. Often, the offers are three months of Audible for $9.99. This discount is an extremely inexpensive promotion that serves to introduce your audience to audiobooks and Audible. Use caution, though, as many of these promotions are only open to people who are not current Audible members.

Gift Memberships for Audible
Even if you don't find a discounted membership, gift memberships are always great prizes or gifts. For $45, a new member receives three months of Audible. The nice thing is, if the listener who receives the gift is already an Audible member, they get three downloads available to them immediately. If you have an audience made up of Audible members, this is a good way to go if you want to do giveaways. Not only do they love it, but it encourages audiobook purchasing.

Audiobook Codes
After publishing your book to Audible, ACX will send the author (and narrator in the case of RS projects) promo codes to giveaway for reviews or promotions. Reviews, just like in the ebook world, get the retailer algorithms moving. If you run out of codes, you can write to ACX support, and they may give you more. Authors encourage narrators to pass out their codes because it costs them nothing and can help you significantly in receiving more reviews.

OneBook
Audible allows readers to gift a book to one person, one time. Encourage your listeners to do this because it's more exposure for you—more word of mouth. Many Facebook audiobook groups contain threads where people can request a OneBook for a specific title from another listener.

Whispersync
Promote Whispersync in audio groups. Many readers love a bargain. When authors put their books on sale or even offer them for free, readers can add the audio narration for just a few dollars more.

Review and Advertising Sites
Audiobook Boom – http://audiobookboom.com/
Audiobook Boom—created, moderated, and run by a long-term, successful audiobook narrator. In exchange for free ACX codes, listeners agree to leave honest reviews of your titles. The cost of this service is only $10 per title, and the moderator keeps a spreadsheet, which is frequently updated, of reviewers who ask for codes but don't leave reviews. He shares that with the people who pay for his service, so they can avoid wasting their codes on consumers who want the free audiobooks but don't want to provide reviews or on those who provide rote reviews.

Audavoxx – http://audavoxx.com/
Audavoxx is very inexpensive service targeted at audiobook lovers. The site is run by Cheri Lacosta, who is a big audiobook advocate. She keeps her advertising prices reasonable and is always dreaming up new ways to get audiobooks in front of the readers who enjoy them. Audavoxx also has a service for distributing ACX codes to avid audio listeners.

Audiofile Magazine – http://www.audiofilemagazine.com
A magazine that offers advertising opportunities, reviews, and information.

Blog Tours
- Book Enthusiast – http://www.bookenthusiastpromotions.com/

Audiobook Blogs
- Dee's Book Blog – https://deesbookblog.com/
- The Literate Housewife – http://literatehousewife.com/
- Eargasms Audiobook Reviews – http://www.eargasmsaudiobookreviews.com/
- Aural Fixation – http://auralfixationaudio.com
- Kris and Vik's Book Therapy Cafe – http://www.krisandvikbooktherapycafe.com/category/reviews/audio-reviews/
- Armchair Audies – https://armchairaudies.com/
- Jacqueline's Reads – http://jacquelinesreads.blogspot.com/p/audio-books.html

Networking/Industry Organizations
Organizations like the Romance Writers of America and the Audio Publishers Association each hold annual conferences, workshops, and mixers throughout the year. Many industry organizations have local

chapters you can join. Attending conferences is an excellent way to network with other authors and narrators.

- ▶ Audio Publishers Association – https://www.audiopub.org/
- ▶ Romance Writers of America – https://www.rwa.org/
- ▶ SAG/AFTRA – http://www.sagaftra.org/

Fundraising Platforms

Some authors and some genres have been successful raising funds to cover their audiobook production costs. Two popular platforms are:

- ▶ Kickstarter – https://www.kickstarter.com/
- ▶ Patreon – https://www.patreon.com/

Book Back Matter

Authors, remember to include your audiobooks in your book back matter. Many times authors forget to mention their audiobooks specifically or include links in their ebook versions.

Backlist

Just like in print publishing, the more audiobooks you have available, the more sales you generate. Have a plan for your backlist. Get all of your books on audio, if possible. Readers will often finish an author's entire backlist before moving onto another.

Affiliate Accounts

Authors and narrators can also sign up for affiliate accounts through Amazon and other retailers to help monetize their websites and promotions. Participating retailers give the affiliate a percentage of sales bought using their unique affiliate link. Even though these are not true royalties, it is another revenue stream that works in tandem with the author and narrator platform. Renea is paid more from her affiliate links than she does from her small press publisher each month. This supplemental income can help offset the cost of advertising.

Talk About the Book

Promote the book to your potential listeners on your social media. Tell people what you love about it or why they should listen to it. Nothing sells more books than a listener's passion.

Join Us

We love to foster a great sense of community for both authors and narrators. In that spirit, here are some resource pages to help you continue your journey. For more information and additional resources, visit us at...

- http://reneamason.com/audiobooks/
- http://www.erindeward.com/narrator-info.html
- http://www.noahmichaellevine.com/narrator-info.html

WHEN THINGS GO WRONG

IF YOUR PARTNER DISAPPEARS

NARRATOR CANCELING CONTRACT

AUTHOR CANCELING CONTRACT

CANCELATIONS WITH FEES ATTACHED
PFH CONTRACTS
RS CONTRACTS

REMOVING A ROYALTY SHARE
AUDIOBOOK FROM RETAIL

WE DON'T LIKE TO THINK ABOUT THIS, AND MAYBE THAT'S why we left it to the end. Sort of like in the book "What to Expect When You're Expecting" where the writers left all of the horrible things that can go wrong during your pregnancy till the very end of the book after they got through all the cool stuff that happens. Sometimes, things go wrong. Maybe it's that the author and the narrator just can't work well together. Maybe the author can't stand the work the narrator did on the book and wants to have it re-done. ACX addresses all of these types of scenarios. These are their current production standards as at the writing of this book: http://www.acx.com/help/production-standard-terms/200485540.

But for the sake of keeping you informed, we share the following:

If for some reason either the author or the narrator wishes to cancel a contract, it isn't complicated to do. First, they will need to confer with each other. Even in the ending of relationships, there has to be clear, consistent, and compassionate communication and agreement that the project will not go forward.

All contract cancelations are reviewed and approved by the ACX Rights department, so one of you will need to email them at info@acx.com using the email address associated with your ACX account. The email should contain your name, the request for cancelation, and the reason for the dissolution. ACX further requests you CC your soon to be ex-partner on this email, so it is clear both parties are interested in ending the contract. As in most things, consent must be clear and mutual for the request to be processed.

IF YOUR PARTNER DISAPPEARS
IF YOU HAVE DONE EVERYTHING IN YOUR POWER TO GET IN touch with them, both through the ACX email system and through regular email, but to no avail, you will want to forward copies of your attempts to info@acx.com and explain the contract cannot proceed since one of the partners has ceased communications. The lovely and helpful people at ACX can work with you to help you dissolve the contract.

NARRATOR CANCELING CONTRACT

A NARRATOR MAY CANCEL THE CONTRACT IF THE AUTHOR does not provide a recordable manuscript within three business days after the offer is accepted.

A narrator may also cancel if the word count of the document is more than 20% or less than 20% of the actual length of the book. In this case, the narrator must notify ACX no later than the date the narrator is due to deliver TFF minutes of the audiobook for approval or the date fifteen days following the date of the Deal Confirmation Page, whichever first occurs.

AUTHOR CANCELING CONTRACT

IF THE NARRATOR DOES NOT DELIVER TFF OR THE FINISHED audiobook by their respective contract dates, the author should make a request, through the ACX email system, for them to do so. If the narrator does not comply within 48 hours, the author may cancel the contract.

CANCELATIONS WITH FEES ATTACHED

AN AUTHOR MAY CANCEL THE CONTRACT BY WRITING TO the narrator using the ACX mail system and should copy to info@acx. com at any time during the raw recording of the book, meaning before any editing or mastering is done. However, these kinds of cancelations are subject to termination fees.

PFH Contracts

The author must pay the narrator a fee equal to 50% of the estimated production fee listed on the original Deal Confirmation Page.

In other words, the audiobook was estimated at ten hours at a PFH rate of $200. The narrator has recorded five hours. The fee would be $1000.

RS Contracts

The author must pay a fee equal to $100 base plus $100 PFH times the projected number of finished hours (in ten-minute increments) listed on the original Deal Confirmation Page; up to a maximum of $2,500.

For example, the book is estimated at ten hours. The fee would be $100 PFH ($1,000) plus $100 base for a total of $1,100.

An author may not fire a narrator after the narrator has completed the initial raw recording of the entire audiobook.

REMOVING A ROYALTY SHARE AUDIOBOOK FROM RETAIL

IT CAN BE DONE, BUT IT ISN'T AS EASY AS JUST DISSOLVING a contract. The contract is for seven years. If the author wants to pull the audiobook down, the narrator must be compensated. ACX has a section on this, specifically, but here's a synopsis:

All communication between the parties regarding the issue should be done through the ACX email system, so that ACX/Audible has access to the chain of events. Since the narrator will be the one most negatively affected by the withdrawal, a compensation agreement needs to be reached between the author and narrator.

Once that's done, consent must be given, in writing, by both parties, to the ACX Rights Team. ACX/Audible will review the request. They may, or may not agree to remove the title.

ONE LAST WEIRD SITUATION

IF AN AUTHOR AND NARRATOR HAVE CONTRACTED UNDER an RS agreement and the audiobook does not get put on sale within nine months after the date the narrator uploads the completed audiobook to ACX, for any reason, other than Audible's rejection due to quality issues or failure to comply with the Production Standard Terms, the narrator will accept a cancelation fee, payable by ACX, equal to $100 times the actual number of finished hours (rounded in ten-minute increments) listed on the Deal Confirmation Page, up to a maximum of $2,500.

We told you this part would be no fun, but we would have been remiss in not including it. For the actual legal terms set out by ACX please visit:

http://audible-acx.custhelp.com/app/answers/detail/a_id/7095/kw/legal

IN CLOSING

WE'VE COME A LONG WAY IN THE ROUGHLY 150 YEARS SINCE Thomas Edison invented the phonograph and recorded Mary Had a Little Lamb. Through a combination of technology, ingenuity, and pure imagination, an industry has grown and flourished. A new breed of storytellers have been born and raised from the wonderful books that preceded them, and a whole new way for authors and actors to increase their presence, fan base, and income streams has evolved and taken its rightful place in the realm of the arts.

If you're new to the world of audiobooks, we hope we have answered some questions and encouraged you to ask even more. We hope our story has been useful to you in creating your own journey. If you've been at this for a while, maybe you've gleaned some new ideas and are inspired to reach out and share with others.

So, join us on this quest. Spread the word. Share the knowledge. Tell your stories—on the page and through the headphones. Get organized. Make a plan. Gather together and support each other. Collaborate. Fascinate. Titillate. But don't procrastinate.

We three found each other, worked out the kinks while talking about the kinky. Plotted a course, talked things through, and successfully produced a whole bunch of audiobooks that our fans seem to love. You can do that, too. You just have to take the first step.

XOXO
Renea, Noah, & Erin

THANK YOU!

Thank you for taking us on your audiobook journey!

As you know, reviews are important and help make books successful. Please consider leaving an honest review on any of the major retailers and review sites.

Your time and feedback is greatly appreciated.

RENEA MASON

"Sexy, fun and so creative it makes my head spin! I'd read the damn phone book if Renea Mason wrote it."

—NYT & USA TODAY Bestselling author ROBYN PETERMAN

Bestselling and multi-award-winning author Renea Mason writes erotic romances which challenge the definition of conventional love. Whether it be contemporary or paranormal, the author of the 2016 Audie Award-winning Curing Doctor Vincent, prides herself on bringing readers unique storylines, memorable characters, and top-notch audiobook performances in her tales of love, lust, and mystery.

In addition to being an author, Renea has spent more than two decades in leadership roles, from manager to vice president, in various fundraising and healthcare organizations. Currently, she works under her legal name, Sheila Hollums Bates, as a Senior Business Advisor, providing management and process consulting services to internal constituencies for the seventh largest revenue producing company in the US.

When she isn't crafting sensual stories which stimulate the mind and body alike or providing the latest management and process guidance, she spends time in the Laurel Mountains of Western Pennsylvania with her beyond-supportive husband, two wonderful sons, and two loving but needy cats.

Renea loves connecting with her readers. Visit her on...

▸ Website – http://ReneaMason.com
▸ Facebook – http://www.facebook.com/ReneaMasonAuthor
▸ Twitter –@reneamason1
▸ Instagram – @renea_mason
▸ YouTube – http://www.youtube.com/c/ReneaMason
▸ SoundCloud – https://soundcloud.com/reneamason

NOAH MICHAEL LEVINE

Noah Michael Levineis an Audie Award-winning narrator, actor and author, living in the beautiful Hudson River Village of Nyack, NY. He has narrated 200 audiobook titles and looks forward to doing many more. He truly loves his work.

Sometimes known by #AuralSexpert, he's performed a lot of Romance and Erotica, but his catalog spans the full breadth of genres, from history, philosophy, science, and literary critique to drama, comedy, young adult, and thriller. He is deeply thankful for and grateful to both Audible and ACX, as well as the authors and lovers of audiobooks who make his work possible.

Noah's career in the entertainment industry spans over thirty years, including a long run as lead singer, lyricist, and keyboard player for the largely unknown 1980s-era band PLCourage and as owner of Eleuthra Productions. He's appeared in many productions from stage to TV and Film, in addition to writing and producing works for large and small screens.

When not in "The Booth," he's an avid home chef, lover of animals and is working on his first novel.

- ▶ Website – http://NoahMichaelLevine.com
- ▶ ACX Narrator Profile –
  https://www.acx.com/narrator?p=A7143UD7LOGB0
- ▶ Facebook – https://www.facebook.com/TheNoahMichaelLevine/
- ▶ Twitter – @badnoah
- ▶ Instagram – @therealbadnoah
- ▶ YouTube – http://www.youtube.com/eleuthra
- ▶ SoundCloud – http://www.soundcloud.com/eleuthra

ERIN DEWARD

Erin deWard is an Audie Award-winning narrator with over fifty titles in genres ranging from Spirituality to Young Adult to Adult Contemporary and others. She's worked on stage, screen, and behind the mic for over thirty years. She is beyond grateful to have come to this place in her life and thanks all of the people and organizations that sped her on her way.

In addition to her love of acting, Erin is passionate about her work as an audio describer, translating visual images in media and performance into aural pictures for people who have low or no vision. She studies and performs Shakespearean text and can most frequently be seen cavorting onstage with The Strange Bedfellows, the adult troupe of the Children's Shakespeare Theatre of New York.

Erin lives in lovely Nyack on Hudson, New York with her husband, daughter, sometimes her college-aged son, and two ill-behaved but loveable dogs, Annie and Benevolio.

- ▶ Website – http://www.erindeward.com/
- ▶ ACX Narrator Profile – https://www.acx.com/narrator?p=AH3BT52XGHXP3
- ▶ Facebook – https://www.facebook.com/erindewardaudiobooks/
- ▶ Twitter – @erindeward

▶ Instagram – @erindeward
▶ SoundCloud – https://soundcloud.com/erin-deward

Made in the USA
Coppell, TX
01 October 2023

22268383R10115